RISORGIMENTO

Also by Lucy Riall

Garibaldi: Invention of a Hero

Sicily and the Unification of Italy, 1859–1866: Liberal Policy and Local Power

Napoleon's Legacy: Problems of Government in Restoration Europe
(edited with David Laven)

RISORGIMENTO

The History of Italy from Napoleon to Nation-state

LUCY RIALL

palgrave
macmillan

First published 2009 by
PALGRAVE MACMILLAN

Palgrave Macmillan in the UK is an imprint of Macmillan Publishers Limited, registered in England, company number 785998, of Houndmills, Basingstoke, Hampshire RG21 6XS.

Palgrave Macmillan in the US is a division of St Martin's Press LLC, 175 Fifth Avenue, New York, NY 10010.

Palgrave Macmillan is the global academic imprint of the above companies and has companies and representatives throughout the world.

Palgrave® and Macmillan® are registered trademarks in the United States, the United Kingdom, Europe and other countries.

ISBN-13: 978–0–230–21669–3   hardback
ISBN-10: 0–230–21669–2   hardback
ISBN-13: 978–0–230–71670–9   paperback
ISBN-10: 0–230–21670–6   paperback

This book is printed on paper suitable for recycling and made from fully managed and sustained forest sources. Logging, pulping and manufacturing processes are expected to conform to the environmental regulations of the country of origin.

A catalogue record for this book is available from the British Library.

Library of Congress Cataloging-in-Publication Data
Riall, Lucy, 1962–
   Risorgimento : the history of Italy from Napoleon to nation state / Lucy Riall.
      p. cm.
   Includes index.
   ISBN 978–0–230–21669–3
   1. Italy—History—1815–1870. 2. Italy—History—1815–1870—
   Historiography. 3. Nationalism—Italy—History—19th century. I. Title.
   DG551.R486 2009
   945' .083—dc22   2008038421

10 9 8 7 6 5 4 3 2 1
18 17 16 15 14 13 12 11 10 09

Printed and bound in China

Contents

List of Maps

List of Figures

More recently, all this has changed again. Since the late 1990s, new analyses of the political economy of the Risorgimento and of Risorgimento culture, influenced in part by the 'linguistic turn' and the development of the new cultural history, have revitalised the study of Risorgimento nationalism and posed new questions about its origins, formation and appeal. This new cultural approach, perhaps most clearly outlined in *Storia d'Italia. Annali 22. Il Risorgimento*, the collection of essays edited by Alberto Banti and Paul Ginsborg and published in 2007, points to the central importance of nationalist ideas and culture in nineteenth-century Italy, and to their impact on the lives, experiences and *mentalités* of Italian men and women.

The present book takes account of all these recent changes in the history of the Risorgimento. In the chapters that follow, I first describe and analyse the implications of the various shifts in historical interpretation; I then outline the main conclusions of historical research and show how these reflect (or fail to reflect) on the problem of national unification. In chapter 1, I sketch out the main events of the Risorgimento from old regime to unification, while in chapters 6 and 7 I address directly the question of Italian nationalism and Italian unification and propose a new interpretation of both. In chapters 2, 3, 4 and 5, I deal in turn with the historiography of the Risorgimento and with Restoration government, society and economy (these chapters are based partly on material published in my 1994 book, *The Italian Risorgimento. State, Society and National Unification*). Each chapter stands alone and can be read separately. However, the themes common to all of them are the rapid changes which swept the Italian peninsula during the early 1800s, the different responses to these changes and how these changes have been explained and understood by historians.

In writing this book, I have been lucky enough to participate in seminars, conferences and informal discussions with the new group of historians in Italy who work on the Risorgimento, and who have so generously welcomed the presence of a non-Italian in their midst. Equally, I have benefited greatly from the presence of an international network of Risorgimento scholars based mainly in France, Britain and the USA. In particular, this book owes a great deal to the series of dialogues and disagreements about the

Risorgimento which I have enjoyed over recent years with Alberto Banti and Paul Ginsborg, and I am very grateful to both of them for their encouragement and advice. I would also like to thank Roberto Balzani, Catherine Brice, John Davis, John Dickie, Christopher Duggan, Maurizio Isabella, Axel Körner, David Laven, Adrian Lyttelton, Marco Meriggi, Nelson Moe, Silvana Patriarca, Gilles Pécout, Marta Petrusewicz and Carlotta Sorba for stimulating many of the themes and ideas outlined in this book, and for making it so much fun to work on nineteenth-century Italy. I am especially indebted to Maurizio Isabella for his valuable comments on chapter 6. My thanks also to the anonymous readers of an earlier version of this book who made some very helpful suggestions for improvement, and to Kate Haines at Palgrave for being such a supportive editor. Nevertheless, nobody but me is responsible for what follows.

1

Risorgimento, Reform and Revolution

The origins of the Risorgimento

Towards the end of the eighteenth century, many of Europe's most powerful monarchies suffered a series of setbacks. Political opposition grew, fed in some places by economic problems and in others by resistance to government policy. In the Habsburg Empire, Joseph II's attempts at large-scale reform severely damaged relations between the crown and the various nobilities of his empire; while in France, the absence of reform and a costly war with Britain led to government bankruptcy and a slow slide into political crisis which culminated spectacularly in the revolution of 1789. In this way, the era of 'Enlightened Absolutism' concluded in a clamour of protest against the governments of Europe's old regime.

It is precisely in this Europe-wide crisis of the eighteenth century that we must look for the origins of the changes in nineteenth-century Italy. From as early as the seventeenth century, most of the city-republics, duchies and kingdoms into which the peninsula was divided had experienced a notable decline relative to their more powerful neighbours. During the course of the seventeenth century much of Italy was ravaged by war and repeated foreign invasion; and some states (the Duchy of Milan, Tuscany and the Kingdom of Naples) came directly under the domination of foreign monarchies. Along with foreign wars, Italy was affected by periodic famines, plagues and popular revolts. However, efforts made by some governments in the eighteenth century to reverse this decline, to introduce economic and social improvements and to construct more efficient bureaucracies and armies, encountered serious difficulties. Attempts to increase state revenue by raising taxes proved unpopular and often unsuccessful. Both the Church and the nobility opposed government attacks on their privileges and traditional powers. Growing social unrest further undermined political stability.

Especially in the Kingdom of Naples, government efforts to commercialise agriculture by abolishing feudal powers (part of a more general attack on noble and clerical privileges), and by encouraging the growth of an agrarian middle class, ran rapidly into political trouble. Despite the consensus among some ministers and many intellectuals in favour of reform, the government was incapable of implementing its reform programme thanks to the opposition of local power-holders. The poor of the countryside bore the brunt of economic change, and the rapid growth of population increased their problems still further. From the 1760s onwards, outbreaks of popular violence became commonplace in many parts of the southern Italian countryside, and these were often encouraged by the nobility and the Church in an attempt to frustrate government reforms.

Some attempts at reform met with greater success, for example in the Duchy of Milan or in Tuscany where the governments had the advantage of more compact territories and relatively more efficient bureaucracies. Moreover, in these states many among the ruling elites agreed on the need for reform. Nevertheless, whether reform was successful or not, it invariably unleashed a process of change which led to instability across the peninsula. The reformers proved quite unable to construct new bases of support or stable relations of power to replace those of the old regime which they had sought to destroy, and had succeeded in weakening. A creeping disillusionment with Italy itself, a distrust of its entrenched political interests and its traditional societies, became a feature of debates about reform even before the cataclysmic events of the 1790s.

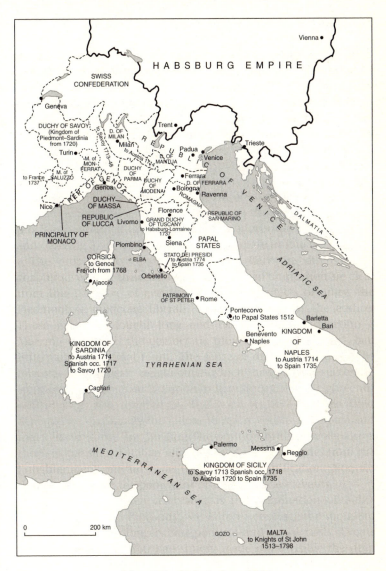

Map 1.1 Italy before 1796

The French Revolution and Napoleon

In 1793 the armies of the French Revolution invaded Piedmont, and occupied its western provinces of Nice and Savoy. In 1796 a new army, reorganised by the young Corsican general Napoleon Bonaparte, invaded northern Italy once more; and with the conclusion of the treaty of Campoformio with Austria in 1797, France gained control of the entire peninsula. These events threw Italy into a period of radical change, as extraordinary as it was complex. From here on until the defeat of Napoleon in 1814, political developments in the peninsula were largely determined by the sequence of victories and defeats experienced by the French armies in a series of wars against Austria, Prussia, Russia and Great Britain.

The French occupations of Italy can be divided into two periods. The first, the Jacobin or Revolutionary 'triennium', lasted from 1796 until 1799. A series of republics were established: in northern Italy the Cispadane and the Transpadane Republics, united in 1797 as the Cisalpine Republic; in central Italy the Roman Republic; and in southern Italy the Parthenopean or Neapolitan Republic. These republics were constantly under threat from France's enemies and from internal opposition; and after the French defeat at the hands of the Second Coalition, they all collapsed and Italy's rulers were briefly restored. Soon afterwards, however, following Napoleon's seizure of power in Paris, the French armies launched a counter-attack in Italy and defeated Austria once more at the battle of Marengo. With the treaty of Lunéville in 1801, Austria recognised French domination of the peninsula. After the defeat of the Third Coalition in 1805, only the islands of Sicily and Sardinia remained outside French control; here the Bourbon royal family (Sicily) and the Savoy royal family (Sardinia) took refuge under the protection of the British navy.

Unlike the Jacobin triennium, when republics were founded, the second, longer period of French occupation (1801–14) was based on monarchical rule, reflecting the conservative direction taken by Napoleon in France. Once he had gained domination of Italy, Napoleon also set about its territorial and administrative reorganisation. Three general territorial divisions were established in Italy. Piedmont and a large part of central Italy (including Rome) were directly annexed by France. A Republic of Italy was created in the north-east in 1802; but after Napoleon's self-proclamation as French Emperor the republic was reconstituted as the Kingdom of Italy, with Napoleon's brother-in-law Eugène de Beauharnais as viceroy, and its territories were gradually expanded to include Istria in the east, Trentino to the north, and the Marche to the south. Finally, in southern Italy, Napoleon established the Kingdom of Naples in 1806, with his brother Joseph as its first sovereign. When Joseph left Naples to become king of Spain in 1808, Napoleon placed his sister Caroline and brother-in-law Joachim Murat on the throne.

Murat's reign in Naples was noteworthy for a number of reasons, not least for his reliance on the support of local elites to assert his kingdom's autonomy from France. When Napoleon's hold over Europe began to waver in 1812, following his defeat in Russia, Murat came to an agreement with the allies to declare war on Napoleon's forces in Italy. But his attempt to ensure the survival of his kingdom by playing a double game with both the allies and Napoleon could not withstand the swings of diplomacy and war. Murat was allowed to keep his throne after Napoleon's first defeat in 1814, but when he decided to support his brother-in-law after the latter's escape from Elba the following year, he made a fatal mistake. Following Napoleon's defeat, Murat was caught in Calabria by Bourbon troops and was executed by firing squad. His death marks the end of French government in the Italian peninsula although not, as we shall see, of its influence over Italian politics.

It would be hard to overestimate the importance of the French occupation for future developments in Italy. In various ways, the experience of the Jacobin years in the late 1790s, and either annexation to France or the creation of satellite kingdoms after 1802, represented a profound break with the past and a powerful harbinger of future hopes and conflicts. The rapid and repeated territorial changes described above worked to undermine the sense of history and of regional difference which had helped to legitimate Italy's old dynasties. By eradicating the existing boundaries of Italy's ten states and overthrowing their governments, and creating in their place three entirely new states with new monarchs and different loyalties, Napoleon challenged the traditional authority and right to rule of the old regime. Less spectacularly, but just as important, the French introduced fiscal and commercial reforms and new communications, all of which aimed to create standardised markets and so ignored or destroyed previous territorial divisions. If only in these ways, the French invasions prepared some of the ground for the development of a more uniform, national identity in Italy.

There were other significant changes too. In particular, the French occupation of the 1790s encouraged the spread of revolutionary ideas and organisations. Even before 1796, Jacobinism had arrived in Italy via the activities of masonic lodges; thereafter, the number of Jacobin or 'patriots" clubs grew rapidly. Encouraged by the economist Melchiore Gioia, the idea of an independent Italian republic gathered support as did calls for democratic forms of government, and, from 1796, the Italian patriots began to plan a series of republican conspiracies and uprisings all over Italy. Yet their freedom of action was always constrained by French control and French priorities. In fact, just as Jacobinism began to gather strength in Italy there was a change of government in France, and the more moderate Directory severely curtailed their energetic efforts and revolutionary experiments. As early as 1797, Napoleon began to repress Jacobin organisations in northern Italy.

The Jacobin-patriots represented a new generation of politically engaged revolutionaries. Although their efforts to change the way Italy was governed were unsuccessful, they became an important (positive and negative) inspiration for future generations after the Revolutionary and Napoleonic wars were over. Even during their short period of political prominence, moreover, they revolutionised political and cultural life in the main cities. Milan rapidly became a centre of political agitation and vibrant press activity. Here, and in other cities, the patriots introduced a new political vocabulary, bringing words like 'nation' and 'fatherland' into public debate. New symbols and rituals were established which made appeals to more participatory forms of political identity and, as part of this process, Italy's past and future became the subject of discussion, while italianità ('Italian-ness') was an inspiration for revolutionary iconography. Thus, the French did not bring nationalism to Italy: that, as we shall see, was the task assumed by a later group of Italians. Nevertheless, their impact on the development of an idea and myth of Italy was decisive.

It is useful to reflect on the failure of the Italian patriots in the French period. One problem was that they never comprised a single movement but were instead a series of groups often divided by bitter disagreements over political action and outlook. Even in the northern Cisalpine Republic where they were strongest, they were split between those who called for radical social reforms to help the poorer classes and those of more moderate tendencies who sought to follow the policies of the Lombard Enlightenment. Besides, although the Jacobins spoke for 'the people', in reality they enjoyed little popular support. Both in the Roman and Neapolitan Republics, the new governments were unable to control large parts of the countryside. The short life of the Neapolitan Republic saw little in the way of practical achievements: indeed, its rulers seemed to fear the power of the large landowners, and they managed only to abolish primogeniture before the regime was abandoned by the French army and the capital, Naples, was invaded by Cardinal Ruffo's counter-revolutionary mob.

In 1799, the republics collapsed amid popular counter-revolution. Led often by local nobles and/or by priests, the counter-revolution was directed against the French and the patriots and made up of armed peasants. Peasant uprisings took place in Tuscany under the banner of the Virgin Mary, and Jacobins were assaulted and killed to the cry of "Viva Maria"; peasant gangs also attacked the Jewish ghettoes in Livorno and Siena. The most aggressive reaction occurred in southern Italy. From Calabria, Cardinal Ruffo put together a huge, unwieldy group of counter-insurgents which he called the Army of the Holy Faith (*Esercito della Santa Fede* or '*sanfedisti*'), with the purpose of defending religion against the 'godless' Jacobins of Naples. Like other counter-revolutionary leaders in Italy and elsewhere, Ruffo played on popular fears and on resentments over taxes and attendant upheavals, blaming peasant hardship on the republican regime in Naples.

Ferocious counter-revolutionary violence (the so-called 'third anarchy') followed the taking of Naples by Ruffo's army. Even Ruffo himself was powerless to control it. Alleged Jacobins were dragged into the street and massacred by the mob; around 8000 people were accused of treason, and more than a hundred republican leaders were executed. The monarchy also entered the fray. Suspecting the

Neapolitan nobility of republican sympathies, it took revenge by abolishing the noble corporations and attempting to replace them with state-controlled administrations. However, the combination of royal revenge and mob violence destabilised the situation still further. Popular revolt and lawlessness spread to, and continued in, the provinces; and the traditional conflict between monarchy and nobility was exacerbated by royal actions. The brutal reconquest of Naples had an important legacy for republicans too. From that moment on, a deep fear of the counter-revolutionary instincts of the peasants and poor, and an implicit desire to keep the masses out of politics, conditioned the political thinking of many republicans in southern Italy and elsewhere.

Just as important for the political future of Italy was the shake-up given to its traditional structures of power. Italy's political, legal and fiscal systems were in truth already quite disturbed by the reforms and accompanying crises of the late eighteenth century; they were then destroyed completely by the revolutionary innovations imported from France. New liberties were created, and more effective forms of state control imposed. This changing relationship between state and society was reflected in the promulgation, during the Jacobin period, of constitutions which introduced elective assemblies. Under Napoleon, sweeping changes were made to centralise and standardise all branches of administration. Attempts were made to introduce new legal codes, feudalism was officially abolished, and the taxation systems were reorganised; and, especially in the north-eastern Kingdom of Italy, the government augmented its revenue with great effectiveness. State power was further increased by the organisation of new police forces (*gendarmerie* or *carabinieri*) and by military conscription. Across Italy, the attack on the political and economic power of the Church was intensified: ecclesiastical lands were put up for sale and the temporal power of the Pope was declared at an end. Religious freedom was introduced, with equal rights given to Jews. New standardised systems of primary, secondary and tertiary education were set up.

In the area of public administration and the army, the impact of Napoleon was equally revolutionary. Here, as in France itself, the particularism and privileges of the old regime bureaucracy were swept away, and officials sought to substitute it with the model of uniform and centralised administration created by the Revolution and implemented by Napoleon. From north to south, the expansion of bureaucracies created new employment opportunities for social groups previously excluded from the corridors of power; the revolutionary concept of a career open to talent (rather to than money or family connections) meant that men from minor noble families and the middle classes now rose rapidly within the ranks of the state bureaucracies. They benefited from, and so supported, Napoleonic rule, just as traditional power-holders resented the encroachment on their particular privileges and tried to resist the French policy of administrative centralisation. A similar process took place within the army, which was greatly expanded throughout the Napoleonic period. So-called 'new men' of relatively humble, middle-class and upper-middle-class backgrounds were admitted as officers in the armies of Napoleon, and were swiftly promoted. Not surprisingly, these officers tended to be fiercely loyal to Napoleon and his new regimes and, like their counterparts in the civil administration, acquired a taste for power in the process of exercising it.

The same cannot be said for Italian peasants. They bitterly resented compulsory military conscription, especially the hardships it brought for their families and the threat it posed to their lives and way of life. Popular protest against the heavy hand of Napoleonic rule, and of the draft in particular, became a commonplace of rural Italy in the years after 1802. In the southern Kingdom of Naples, where the reform programme had anyway been less successful than in the north, full-scale peasant revolt broke out in Calabria in 1806. Helped by British forces, encouraged by the clergy and led by the charismatic brigand Fra' Diavolo, the conflict between the Napoleonic rulers of Naples and the rural poor raged for two years and was accompanied by terrible violence and loss of life.

Peasant reaction, and the alliance between peasants and the Church, was a striking indication of the disruptions caused by the French period in Italy. It reminds us that the Revolutionary and Napoleonic invasions created losers as well as winners, and that the losers could fight back quite successfully. Thus, the modernisation brought by the French may have benefited some, but not everyone, and while the impact of change was irreversible, it was also divisive and destabilising. This struggle between those who embraced change and those who resisted it, and between the manifest need for reform and the need to control its consequences, was also to characterise political debate in Italy during the decades following the fall of Napoleon.

Restoration (1815–30)

After the defeat of Napoleon in 1814/15, the Congress of Vienna set out to restore the rulers of *ancien régime* Europe, along with most of their territories and former boundaries. In Italy, the Restoration was strictly defined and controlled by the Habsburg Empire, France's long-term adversary in the peninsula. Not surprisingly, Austrian domination of Italy was guided by the opposition to constitutional government felt by the so-called 'Great Powers' at Vienna, associated as it was with the slide into revolutionary violence and war, and by a corresponding desire to bolster up the political and moral foundations (the 'legitimacy') of absolute rule. At the same time, the Italian Restoration was strongly influenced by foreign policy considerations. 'It is on the River Po that we defend the Rhine', remarked the Austrian Chancellor, Prince Clemens von Metternich: the clear priority was to maintain the balance of power in Italy, which in practice meant a commitment to keeping France out and Austria in control.

So Italy's territorial settlement reflected its role as a pawn in European diplomacy. Unsurprisingly, the settlement was determined more by Austria's rivalry with France than it was by any aspiration to help Italy's rulers recover their traditional powers. Under the terms of the Vienna treaty, Lombardy was returned to Austria, and the former Venetian Republic (abolished by Napoleon) was not restored but also incorporated into the Habsburg Empire; Austrian control was also confirmed by the arrangements for the Grand Duchy of Tuscany and the Central Italian Duchies of Modena and Parma, all of which were ruled by members of the Habsburg dynasty. In central and southern Italy, the Restoration was more straightforward: the Papal States (including the northern

Legations, separated from papal rule for most of the French period) were returned to the Pope; and the Kingdom of Naples, with the island of Sicily, was returned to its absolute ruler, Ferdinando IV (who renamed his kingdom the Kingdom of the Two Sicilies, and took the new name Ferdinando I). Both the Pope and Ferdinando I made concessions to Austrian power in Italy, and expected Austrian help in the event of external or internal aggression. Ferdinando signed a permanent defensive alliance with Austria, which gave Austria the effective right to intervene militarily in his kingdom; while the Pope allowed the Austrian army a permanent military garrison in the city of Ferrara.

After 1815, only the Kingdom of Sardinia remained relatively independent of Austria. Piedmont, as it is usually known, was actually made stronger by the incorporation of the Genoese Republic on its Mediterranean coast. Yet, as we shall see, however vital this independence proved to be for the future of Italy, it was not the result of Piedmont's military and political clout in Europe but rather due to its strategic position on the French border. At Vienna, Piedmont was simply conceived of as a 'buffer-state' between France and Austria, and it lacked the material force to provide any kind of counter-weight to Austrian power in the peninsula. Nor did Piedmont initially conceive of any such role for itself. Although anti-Austrian sentiment was widespread and increasing among the ruling elite in Piedmont, and while anti-Austrianism offered a potential source of support for the Savoy monarchy, there were few if any signs that Piedmont identified its political interests with those of Italian independence in general.

The policies and problems of Italy's Restoration governments are the subject of chapter 3. Here it is worth noting that the term 'Restoration' masked a variety of different attitudes and forms: from the relatively liberal, consensual programme pursued by prime minister Fossombroni in Tuscany to the out-and-out reaction of Vittorio Emanuele I in Piedmont and Francesco IV in the Duchy of Modena. These varieties notwithstanding, the Restoration in Italy was almost everywhere marked by considerable protest and resistance from almost all sections of the elites as well as by the poor. Resistance was partly a European phenomenon: not just in Italy, but in France, Spain and the German states too, the authority

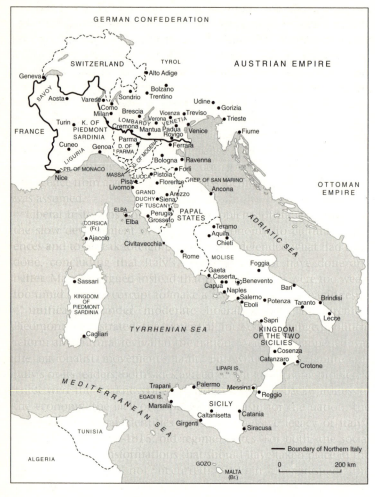

Map 1.2   Italy in 1815

of the restored rulers had been severely undermined by the traumatic experiences of revolution and war. The traditional elites expected much more from the Restoration, that is, the restitution of all their powers, including those taken away during the eighteenth-century reforms; while the 'new men' who had rose to power under Napoleon were just as angered by their demotion, and sometimes outright dismissal, following the return of the old monarchies. Popular unrest, such a feature of the French years, continued after Napoleon's fall. Indeed, a bad famine in 1817 and the need of all rulers to maintain a high level of taxes led to the constant threat and fear of unrest.

It was just this atmosphere of political instability and economic unrest which benefited the 'secret societies' or sects. These revolutionary groups – such as the *carboneria* and the *adelfia* – had formed originally in opposition to the authoritarianism of the Napoleonic regimes. They had been encouraged in the early 1800s by the British and Austrians as a way of undermining French rule, though in Naples the carbonari grew especially in importance because Murat decided to encourage them. In the aftermath of Napoleon's defeat, the secret societies spread and proliferated. Their members were in turn, however, to be disappointed by the conservatism of the Restoration in Italy, and quickly became involved in conspiracies against the Vienna settlement.

Important as they are for providing continuity between Jacobinism and the later conspiracies of Mazzini's Young Italy, especially through the figure of the old Jacobin leader Filippo Buonarotti, the secret societies had a limited practical impact. They shared few clear political aims, and the need for secrecy meant they were unable to develop a general strategy – although secrecy did little to prevent their organisations from being infiltrated by spies. Nor did the secret societies have much in common with other movements of moderate opposition which developed at around the same time, notably the group of progressive liberals based in Lombardy and grouped around the journal *Il Conciliatore*.

Nevertheless, the obstinate absolutism of some states like Piedmont, and frustration at their lack of influence in others like Lombardy and Tuscany, did push many liberals towards sympathy with the secret societies. In the summer of 1820, a conspiracy among army officers and carbonari members led to a revolution in Naples, obliging King Ferdinando I to grant a constitution; this was quickly followed by a violent uprising in the streets of Palermo, with popular protest at the economic crisis becoming briefly allied both to the separatist ambitions of Sicilian nobles and to the artisans' defence of their corporative privileges. To the north, in Piedmont, concern about events in Naples, led to equally intense plotting among army officers and carbonari and eventually, in March 1821, to a widespread insurrection which declared a constitution and proclaimed an Italian federation as its aim (specifically, calling for Austria to be driven out of Lombardy).

The carbonarist uprisings of 1820–1 were a failure, easily suppressed by the Austrian army acting with local forces and the approval of Europe. Other than Austrian repression, there were a number of reasons for the failure, most obviously the internal disarray among the revolutionaries themselves. Although all were offended by the absolutist regimes, divisions between constitutional moderates and the much more radical democrats, both in the south and in Piedmont, meant that they spent as much time stopping each other as they did working together. In Piedmont, officers led by Santorre di Santarosa supported a coup against King Vittorio Emanuele I, in alliance with revolutionary sects, but liberal moderates like Cesare Balbo feared any sign of overt disloyalty to the throne. In Naples and Sicily, there were further disagreements still. That is, moderates and democrats argued about the extent of reform and whether or not to allow 'the people' into politics, but their differences were complicated by the presence of other interests and loyalties: by Sicilians who resented rule from Naples and, within Sicily, by other provincial elites (especially in Messina and Catania) who objected to the domination of Palermo. In Sicily, moreover, the nobility's rejection of Neapolitan rule was met by rural violence on a scale which nobody welcomed or desired, and this helped to turn the nobility against the revolution.

A notable difference between Piedmont and the Kingdom of the Two Sicilies emerged during the events of 1820–21. Although Austrian help was necessary for the repression of both revolutions, in other respects Piedmont appeared more stable. In Piedmont, left and right agreed over the need to avoid popular disorder and on the basic legitimacy of the Savoy monarchy, so that once the king abdicated in 1821, and was replaced by his brother Carlo Felice, the situation stabilised. Thus, while the revolution in the south revealed the huge extent of political, social and even territorial disaggregation, in Piedmont the revolution revealed elements of a basic, and relatively conservative, consensus. The advantages which this consensus gave to the Piedmontese state were to become more obvious over the next four decades.

Young Italy

A period of political reaction came after the 1820–21 revolutions. In 1831, another wave of revolutionary disturbances swept the peninsula, this time affecting above all the Papal Legations and the central Italian duchies, and the pattern established in 1820–21 can be also discerned in these later events. As soon as the regimes were seen to falter, Italian revolutionaries seized the advantage and threw themselves into conspiratorial action, establishing an illustrious tradition of patriotic martyrdom in the process. But they lacked the necessary organisation and/or the material force ever to hold on to that advantage, to restore order and to resist the inevitable counter-attack and reaction which followed. As in previous uprisings, moreover, the mass of the people remained indifferent or openly hostile to the call to revolt.

More important than the revolutions themselves was the fallout thereafter. On the government side, Austrian intervention to crush the revolutions did little to restore political authority or to control the tide of popular hostility which continued to mount after the revolutions were over: in Bologna, for example, repeated uprisings against the papal administration obliged the Austrians to retain a garrison there until 1838. So the revolutions discredited the governments of central Italy, and showed just how shallow their legitimacy was. On the other side, the side of the revolutionaries, matters were just as bad. Political moderates were disgraced by the timid, even equivocal, attitude which they had maintained throughout the revolutionary events, while the democrats proved plainly incapable: unable to take the initiative or organise a practical movement. The revolutions also signalled the political end of the old conspirator Filippo Buonarotti, whose vain attempt to organise an expedition in France to help the Italian insurrections was blocked by the French government.

The disarray of the revolutionary forces in 1831 is worth stressing, because out of it a new movement emerged. This movement was 'Young Italy' (*Giovine Italia*) led by an ex-*carbonaro*, Giuseppe Mazzini. Mazzini had been arrested for carbonari conspiracies before the revolutions broke out, and by 1831 had left Italy for France; the disastrous experiences of these years convinced him that it was necessary to create an entirely new kind of leadership which would prepare the ground for the battle to come. In particular, he rejected the carbonarist dependence on France for inspiration and direction, and argued that the future belonged to an organisation which did not subordinate Italian interests to those of the foreigner and would realise Italy's historic mission to put itself at the head of the movement for the liberation of all nations. Mazzini's achievements will be assessed more fully in chapter 6: here we will concentrate on the early part of his career (until 1848–49).

Mazzini's muse was different from that of the carbonari, and the Jacobins before them. Like many young men and women of his generation, he was inspired by the prevailing mood of melancholy romanticism and by its emotional engagement with the past. Young Italy was born out of the romantic sense of Italy's past greatness, and by the conviction that the nation was created by God not to be divided and oppressed, as at present, but destined by geography, history and nature to be a free, united nation. Mazzini also sought to emphasise the break with the French Revolution by excluding the over-40s from his organisation, and by its unambiguous, concrete objectives: these were nothing less than the overthrow of every old regime in Italy (including, and perhaps above all, the Papacy), and the creation in its place of a new Italy, united as a democratic republic. With Mazzini, the sense of decline and the hope for renewal, which had driven reformers and revolutionaries alike since the 18th century, became linked to a mystical desire for national resurrection or *risorgimento*.

Between 1831 and 1834, Young Italy rapidly acquired a great notoriety. Its principal means of communication and education

Figure 1.1 Giuseppe Mazzini.

Caldesi, Blanford & Co. albumen carte-de-visite, early 1860s, © National Portrait Gallery, London, UK.

Mazzini is seen in a typical pose, which emphasises both the romantic lone-liness of his London exile and his status as the theorist or 'visionary' of Italian nationalism (alluded to by the window, bookshelves and desk in the background).

was the published word, and Mazzini also tried to organise a series of insurrections in Italy, starting with what he hoped would be a major revolution in Turin and Genoa in 1833–34. Yet despite these initial advances, and Young Italy's undoubted success in intimidating the forces of conservatism and reaction, by the mid-1830s this movement too was in considerable disarray. Before the attempted insurrection in Turin and Genoa could get underway, it was discovered by the authorities, and Mazzini fled to Switzerland in despair. In the crackdown which followed, the Young Italy organisation was badly damaged. Only after he moved to London in 1837, did Mazzini's revolutionary energies begin to recover, although even then it was not until 1840 that he refounded the organisation (this time with a special branch for Italian workers) and began to plan conspiracies once more.

Young Italy was involved in a revolutionary uprising in Bologna in 1843, and associated with the tragic expedition of the Bandiera brothers to the Calabrian coast in 1844. The failed attempt by the latter to spark off a popular revolt among the peasants of Calabria, with a force of some twenty men, indicates both the strengths and weaknesses of the Mazzinian organisation. On the one hand, the expedition failed completely to achieve any of its desired aims: the population did not rise to greet the brothers, as was confidently predicted, and the brothers and their followers were executed by Bourbon troops. The expedition itself was badly armed, infiltrated by spies and had no real knowledge of the territory and inhabitants which it had travelled from Venice to liberate. On the other hand, the brothers' heroic self-sacrifice was admired by contemporaries, and Mazzini's public efforts to celebrate what he called their 'martyrdom' for Italy attracted the attention of radicals across Europe and further afield. So, Mazzinian propaganda turned a political disaster into something of a publicity triumph, and this contributed to an awakening of interest in Italian affairs both among Italians and internationally.

Mazzini also created a broad radical network, centred on London but with links across Europe and to the Americas. Through relentless hype, Mazzini was able to persuade influential British liberals of the justice and inevitability of the Italian cause, and from the 1840s he began to raise significant sums of money from liberal sympathisers for his programme. In the mid-1840s, he also scored a major publicity success with the promotion of Giuseppe Garibaldi, a little-known Italian exile based in Uruguay. Thanks in part to the efforts of Mazzini and his followers, and in part to the liberalisation of press laws in many parts of Italy, Garibaldi became a political celebrity in the years leading up to the outbreak of the 1848 revolutions. Through the press, Mazzini promoted him as a new symbol of the national resurgence which he foresaw for Italy, if only the nation were allowed to overthrow its reactionary and corrupt governments (all these issues are looked at more fully in chapter 6).

By the 1840s, however, Mazzini began to face a challenge of another kind. The moderate liberal movement, which had always condemned his programme as unrealistic and dangerous, began to gather political force in Italy. Although the movement itself had deep roots, both in 18th-century Lombard reformism and in the progressive concerns of the Lombard and Tuscan Restoration, most of its members had little direct involvement in politics, preferring instead to pursue their interests in scientific developments and in historical, literary and artistic questions. But in the 1840s, this began to change. Most notably, with the publication of three overtly political books by prominent moderate liberals – Vincenzo Gioberti's *Of the moral and civil primacy of Italians* (*Del primato morale e civile degli Italiani*, 1843); Cesare Balbo's *The hopes of Italy* (*Delle speranze d'Italia*, 1844); and Massimo d'Azeglio's, *The recent events in Romagna* (*Degli ultimi casi di Romagna*, 1846) – the movement acquired a set of political objectives and an explicitly nationalist dimension.

Gioberti's *Primato* was especially popular and caused a minor publishing sensation. It also opened the way for many moderates in states like Piedmont, Lombardy and Tuscany to become fervent supporters of what was called 'neo-Guelphism'. In the book, Gioberti laid out an alternative proposal for an Italian confederation with the Pope as president, a quite different – and much more conservative – idea than Mazzini's unitary Republic. For the first time, in other words, the moderates had a dynamic political programme to rival that of Mazzini. In 1846, the neo-Guelph project was given added force with the election of the 'liberal Pope'

Pius IX, and subsequently with the seeming endorsement of nationalist aspirations in northern Italy by the Piedmontese king, Carlo Alberto.

By the middle of the 1840s, and especially for the cultural elites of the major cities who mostly despised him, Mazzini's revolutionary aspirations for Italy appeared to be losing ground. In its place rose a more moderate, and much less democratic, form of nationalism which sought a compromise with Italy's monarchs (including the Pope) on the basis of gradual, non-violent reform. Carlo Alberto's turn to liberalism and the nation in Piedmont was then further confirmed by similarly liberal moves undertaken by Leopoldo II in Tuscany, and by the decision of these two sovereigns and the Pope to create a customs' union. During these years, moreover, a vibrant, liberal public opinion emerged and was consolidated: new journals were published, and liberal associations were established, in which the idea of Italy and proposals for political and economic reform were openly discussed. Although the spread of liberalism was uneven (the Duke of Modena remained resolutely reactionary), by 1847 the sense of political expectation was palpable. It was in this atmosphere of confidence and excitement that the traumatic events of 1848 unfolded.

The 'springtime of the peoples' (1848–49)

In January 1848, a major revolt broke out in the centre of Palermo. The army was quickly overcome, and an independent government declared Bourbon rule at an end. By the spring, revolution had crossed the peninsula to Naples, Rome, Bologna, Florence, Livorno, Turin, Milan and Venice, and reached throughout the European continent to Paris, Vienna, Budapest and Berlin. Strikes, riots and demonstrations became commonplace in the major cities of Europe, caused by three years of economic depression and food shortages. Encouraged by radicals, protest spread rapidly thanks also to new forms of communication such as the railway and the telegraph. The effect was to shake the thrones of Europe. After street fighting in Paris, King Louis Philippe abdicated in February; in March, with the city in open revolt, Chancellor Metternich was smuggled out of Vienna. Amid similarly chaotic scenes in Italy, constitutions were granted by the rulers of the Two Sicilies, the Papal States, Tuscany and Piedmont. The revolution in Austrian Venice led to the declaration of a republic by its leader, Daniele Manin, while in neighbouring Lombardy, the population rose up and after five days of fighting (the famous *Cinque Giornate*) threw out the Austrian army and its commander, Field-Marshal Radetsky. In April 1848, Mazzini arrived in Milan to a triumphant welcome.

Yet this dizzying series of events, and the apparent ease of victory over conservatism and reaction, masked some grave weaknesses within the revolutionary forces. The most obvious of these was that only some of them were truly revolutionary. In most Italian states, the moderate liberals gained, or remained, firmly in control of government, and once they had obtained constitutions from their rulers, they sought to halt the revolution, to marginalise the democrats and to prevent 'the masses' from entering politics. In Palermo, the moderates moved against the democrats who had supported popular revolution; and in Lombardy, Venice and Tuscany, political disagreement was a feature of relations between the two sides from the outset. These divisions would have been less serious had it not been for the strength of their political opponents – notably Austria – who despite appearances to the contrary had suffered no more than a temporary setback in northern Italy. In reality, the triumph of revolution was little more than a mirage, and Italian conservatives were merely biding their time before mounting an effective counter-attack.

Then, the moderate liberals proved unable to hold the middle ground between revolution and reaction. First, they badly underestimated the strength of popular discontent in the cities, and equally overestimated their ability to control the unemployed and artisans who had formed the backbone of the revolution in the early months of 1848. Moreover, focused as they were on urban areas, the moderates ignored the situation in the countryside, and offered no solution to the problem of land distribution which had caused successive waves of peasant protest even before the revolutions began. In some states, such as Lombardy, the new leadership introduced military conscription, thus worsening conditions for the peasants. The overall failure to address the causes and consequences of mass unrest had grim political consequences. On the one hand, in Sicily, fear of peasant violence drove the landowners into the arms of the conservatives; faced with the choice between protecting their property and political freedom, they quickly chose the former, abandoning the liberal government in Palermo and supporting the restoration of royal authority. On the other, in Lombardy and Venetia, it was the peasants who feared the revolution and welcomed back the Austrians: as early as the summer of 1848, cries of *'Viva Radetsky!'* greeted Austrian soldiers as they marched across the Lombard countryside to reconquer Milan.

At the same time, Italian monarchs proved obstinately averse to reform and to sharing even the most moderate nationalist ambitions for Italy. Initially, moderates had some reason to be optimistic. In March 1848, Carlo Alberto of Piedmont declared war on Austria, and his army was joined by volunteer forces from the Papal States and Naples. The first battle with the Austrians resulted in a Piedmontese victory. However, the rush of volunteers to fight against Austria, a Catholic power, alarmed the Pope and at the end of April he announced his neutrality in the conflict with Austria, and called the papal volunteers home. Then, in May, Ferdinando II of Naples carried out a coup d'état against the liberals, dissolved parliament and ordered the Neapolitan army to return to the kingdom. So, in the space of three months, the united Italian front against the Austrians was destroyed. Disaster followed. In July, at the battle of Custoza, the Piedmontese army suffered a crushing defeat and, shortly afterwards, Carlo Alberto signed an armistice and retreated behind his borders in Piedmont, abandoning Milan to Radetsky and the Austrian army. At the end of the summer, Ferdinando II sent his army southwards to reconquer Sicily.

The Piedmontese defeat, and the actions of Carlo Alberto, Pope Pius IX and Ferdinando II showed that the trust which moderate liberals had placed in their sovereigns was entirely misplaced. Piedmont's army was no match for the Austrians, the Pope had no interest in Italian nationalism and Ferdinando II was an enemy of the liberals. Neo-Guelphism was a failure. It was at this point that Mazzini seized the initiative back from the moderates. He issued an emotional 'Appeal to Italians', declaring that if the war between kings was over, the war of the people had just become. From July

1848 onwards, the democrats gained the upper hand: in Venice, where the Republic had survived the Austrian conquest of Lombardy, popular support for Manin's leadership remained high; in Rome, following the assassination of the moderate prime minister Pellegrino Rossi and the flight of the Pope to the fortress of Gaeta, the democrats seized control.

Mazzini arrived in Rome in February 1849. A republic was declared in Rome and a constituent assembly was called to discuss the unification of Italy. Universal manhood suffrage was introduced; the tax system was reformed; the Church's control over education was abolished; and Church property was nationalised, and its distribution among the peasantry was announced. In the meantime, in Tuscany, a similarly radical government took power under the democrats Giuseppe Montanelli and Francesco Domenico Guerrazzi. After the Grand Duke Leopoldo abandoned Florence, a democratic republic was declared in Tuscany as well.

Yet circumstances were no more favourable to the democrats in 1849 than they had been to their Jacobin counterparts fifty years earlier. Neither in Tuscany nor in Venice were military preparations made for the defence of the republics; only in Rome, and much too late, did the republic find in Garibaldi a military leader with the ability to organise a counter-attack, but here too his forces were weak and ill-equipped. Nor, despite the reform efforts of the Roman Republic, did the democrats ever succeed in winning over the bulk of the population. Besides, just as the democrats took power in Italy, the counter-revolution gained momentum in the rest of Europe. In April 1849, Austrian domination of the Italian peninsula was reaffirmed once more, with the second decisive defeat of the Piedmontese army at Novara. This victory opened the whole peninsula to the forces of reaction.

After the defeat of Novara, Carlo Alberto abdicated the Piedmontese throne in favour of his son, Vittorio Emanuele II, but the city of Genoa rose in rebellion just the same. After ten days of revolution, the city was bombarded into submission by the Piedmontese navy; in the same period, the Austrian army brutally crushed a popular revolt in the Lombard city of Brescia and commenced a long, equally violent campaign against peasant unrest and brigandage in the lower Lombardy plain. Austria also

Figure 1.2   Giuseppe Garibaldi in Palermo, 1860.

Gustav le Gray, Albumen carte-de-viste, 1860, © National Portrait Gallery, London, UK.

This photograph of Garibaldi was taken at the height of his fame, during his triumphant conquest of Sicily. The hero's relaxed, sensual pose was unusual for the period, as was his casual attire, and both emphasise his rejection of political and military conventions. The photograph provided the basis for countless reproductions in illustrated magazines, and is an indication of Garibaldi's worldwide fame.

intervened against Tuscany. The army occupied the port city of Livorno, known for its radical sympathies, arrested and executed many revolutionary leaders, and restored the Grand Duke to his throne in Florence. Finally, in May, the Bourbon army concluded its long battle to restore royal authority to Sicily when it occupied the capital, Palermo.

So in May 1849, the democrats remained in control only of Rome and Venice. Now Rome came under attack, from Bourbon forces in the South and, more seriously, from a French expeditionary force sent by the new president, Louis Napoleon (the nephew of Napoleon Bonaparte), to protect Catholics and restore the Pope. There followed two months of heroic resistance to the French siege led by Garibaldi and by volunteers from all over Italy, which captured the attention of the world's press. But on 2 July, the outnumbered and outgunned Republic was forced to admit defeat and surrender to the French. With the remainder of his army, Garibaldi tried to march north to help the Venetian Republic, under Austrian siege and in the grip of disease and starvation. His and all other attempts to save Venice failed. The city, the last one in Europe to remain in the hands of the revolution, fell to the Austrians at the end of August.

The 'decade of preparation' (1849–59)

The revolution paid dearly for the fright given to Italian rulers in 1848 and 1849. Ten years of severe repression ensued. Both Pius IX in Rome and Leopoldo II in Tuscany turned their backs on liberalism; they reintroduced censorship and cracked down on any sign of political dissent or discontent. In Lombardy-Venetia, the presence of the Austrian police and military was felt everywhere, and those who had taken part in the revolutions were denounced, arrested, sent into exile or executed. The repressive atmosphere in the Two Sicilies spared no-one: even the most moderate liberals were arrested and condemned to long years in prison, and all cultural and political activities outside the control of the crown were frowned upon and banned. Only in Piedmont did the constitution granted by the king in 1848 live on, guaranteeing basic political and civil liberties and allowing a narrow form of representative government. And it was only in Piedmont that the liberal atmosphere of the pre-'48 period endured, and indeed was given a boost by the increasing numbers of political exiles from elsewhere in Italy who now made Piedmont their home.

The impact of the revolutions of 1848–49 on Italian nationalism will be discussed again in chapter 6. At this point, it is worth stressing that the revolutions were a turning point for both moderates and democrats in Italy. At first, the democrats did well out of the events: Mazzini, Garibaldi and others won widespread international fame as a result of their valiant efforts to fight for a republic, and, despite the defeat, Mazzini expected victory soon. Welcomed as a hero when he returned, as an exile once more, to London, he set up a new 'National Italian Committee' and sought new funds to support the next revolution in Italy. But these early advances were misleading. They were followed by a succession of failed insurrections: Milan in 1853, Massa in 1854, Palermo in 1856 and, worst of all, Carlo Pisacane's expedition to Sapri in 1857. In this last instance, the expedition ended terribly with Pisacane's suicide amid the total indifference of the local population, and the imprisonment or execution of his associates.

The failure of these poorly prepared, badly armed insurrections was not entirely Mazzini's fault, but he received all the blame when the uprisings collapsed, their leaders were captured and a general military crackdown ensued. Although Mazzini's reputation survived in his (now) home city of London, elsewhere his standing declined. The air of failure which attached itself to his activities did little to reassure those already depressed by the experiences of persecution, imprisonment and exile. By the mid-1850s, the democratic movement began to lose both unity and momentum: criticism of Mazzini grew ('the tyrant of our party' according to one former supporter), and a series of dissident organisations took shape in cities like Paris and Genoa where his influence was less strong.

By far the most striking sign of the changing political climate was the establishment in 1857 of the Italian National Society. This was the creation of three democrats, Daniele Manin (ex-leader of the Venetian Republic, exiled in Paris), Giorgio Pallavicino

Trivulzio and Giuseppe La Farina (both living in exile in Turin), and it was based on their conviction that the only way forward for Italian nationalism was through an alliance with Piedmont. In effect, what Manin and the others proposed was that Mazzinians should abandon their commitment to revolution and to an Italian republic, and should instead accept the leadership of Piedmont, its monarchy and its army in a combined struggle to throw out the Austrians and unite the peninsula. National unity, rather than independence and freedom, became the prime objective for these democrats-turned-monarchists. In the years after the founding of the National Society in 1857, the movement gathered strength; it gained a large membership, a newspaper and, most importantly of all, the endorsement of the Piedmontese government.

In truth, what these developments reflected most of all was the changing role of Piedmont. This change was due to its new government after 1849 which, quite unlike anywhere else in Italy, took a decidedly liberal direction. After 1849, with the constitution of 1848 as their starting point, moderate liberals found in Piedmont the compromise between royal authority and liberal reform which had eluded them before. The Piedmontese constitution confirmed the power of the crown and the Church, but it also guaranteed freedom of the press and of association. Above all, it allowed for a parliament, that is, an elective body with the power of making and rejecting legislation and, while its power was always limited by an extremely narrow suffrage (less than 2% of the adult male population) and the royal prerogative, parliament offered moderate liberals an autonomous basis of power. Thus, the success of liberalism in Piedmont was unpredicted and never that secure. Yet from relatively fragile beginnings, the moderate liberals managed to reform the economy and to transform political life, and these impressive achievements formed a striking contrast both to political reaction elsewhere in the peninsula and the political disarray within the democratic movement.

Much of the credit for this remarkable success must go to one man, Camillo Benso di Cavour, who became prime minister of Piedmont in 1852. The second son of a minor noble family, whose father had disgraced himself by supporting Napoleon in the early 1800s, Cavour represented in his person and his outlook both

Italy's complex response to modernisation and the moderate solution to it, which was to steer a path between the twin horrors (as moderates saw them) of revolution and reaction. Cavour despised the Austrians and Mazzini in equal measure, and his real passion was for economic progress which resulted, in his view, from free trade, a liberal polity and political stability. His political models were François Guizot in France and Robert Peel in Britain; he especially admired Peel's attempt to guide the Tory party towards a programme of moderate ('conservative') reform thus stealing the radicals' political energy. In addition, Cavour combined these liberal convictions with a genuine talent as a political tactician. Between 1852 and 1859, he used these gifts to dominate Piedmontese politics and, from this position, to assert Piedmontese power within Italy and the leadership of Italy abroad.

Cavour started out in 1852 by ousting the incumbent prime minister, Massimo d'Azeglio. His support was built on a pact (often called an 'illicit alliance' or *connubio*) between the centre-right and centre-left, and the *connubio* gave him both a constant majority in parliament and a solid power base with which to resist the king's attempts to undermine parliamentary authority. Cavour, in turn, used his control of parliament to attack the Church, a main pillar of reaction in Piedmont. Civil marriage was introduced, and state control over education and over religious appointments was established. In 1855, after a protracted struggle in parliament and between parliament and the king, a law suppressing a number of religious orders was passed.

To the battle against religion Cavour joined a battle for economic growth. Free trade agreements were signed with all the major European powers except for Russia, Piedmont's banking and credit system was standardised and modernised, and huge efforts were made to encourage foreign investment. Perhaps the most striking evidence of economic progress was in the development of modern communications, including telegraph lines, canals and (primarily) railways. Cavour was a great enthusiast for rail travel, and during the 1850s railways in Piedmont increased from a mere 8 kilometres of track in 1849 to an impressive 850 kilometres in 1859 (that is, some 47% of all the railway lines in Italy).

War and diplomacy

The ascendancy of moderate liberalism in Piedmont between 1849 and 1859 is often referred to as 'the decade of preparation'. This phrase reflects the importance of this decade for the growth of Italian nationalism and, eventually, the unification of Italy. As we have seen, the successes of Piedmont contrasted dramatically with the problems of the other Italian states, and the presence of the National Society served to emphasise the legitimacy of Piedmontese leadership over the nationalist struggle. Thanks to the activities of the National Society, Cavour – and even the king Vittorio Emanuele II – became persuaded of the advantages of an alliance with the nationalists. Never an Italian nationalist himself, and strongly opposed to the Mazzinian idea of national unification, Cavour perceived in nationalism the possibility of harnessing its broad appeal to his own political ambitions. These were to eject Austria from northern Italy and make Piedmont the dominant presence in the Lombardy plain (which he correctly recognised to be the future power house of the Italian economy).

Cavour's methods were traditional, but he put them to quite modern ends. He acknowledged the crucial lesson of 1848–49 – that on its own Piedmont could never defeat Austria – and he also saw that diplomacy was the only way to gain an ally for Piedmont and isolate Austria. His abilities as a diplomat became evident during the Crimean War (1853–56), when he persuaded the king to enter the war on the Franco-British side and to have the 'Italian Question' discussed at the peace conference afterwards. From 1856 onwards, he encouraged anti-Austrian agitation in northern and central Italy, and provoked Austria into breaking off diplomatic relations in 1857. His major opportunity came in early 1858, when an ex-Mazzinian extremist, Felice Orsini, threw a bomb at the carriage of the French Emperor (Napoleon III: the former Louis Napoleon) as he travelled to the opera in Paris, claiming as his motive the suffering of Italy and Napoleon's failure to do anything about it. This attack, which Napoleon III survived, had dramatic, and largely unintended, consequences. It further discredited Mazzini (who had little to do with it), it led to problems in France's relations with England and, most surprising of all, it persuaded Napoleon III to seek a rapprochement with Piedmont.

In July 1858, the two statesmen met at the French spa town of Plombières, where they devised an elaborate plan to expel Austria from northern Italy. In return for French help in the war against Austria, Napoleon III demanded the two Piedmontese provinces of Savoy and Nice for France, and a marriage between his nephew, the middle-aged dissolute Prince Jerôme, and the king of Piedmont's daughter, a pious 15-year-old girl named Clotilde. Napoleon also made French military help dependent on Austria declaring war first: only by seeming the aggressor in the war, he insisted, would Austria remain diplomatically isolated and be possible to defeat.

On this basis, the two turned their attention to the map of Italy. In their scheme, at the end of the war Piedmont would be united with Lombardy, Venice and the Papal Legations, and form a Kingdom of Upper Italy; Tuscany would form a separate kingdom with the rest of the Papal States; the Pope would be left with Rome and the surrounding province; while the Kingdom of the Two Sicilies would remain as before. Napoleon III and Cavour also talked of an Italian confederation with the Pope as president, as a consolation for the loss of most of his territory. But the fact was that the two planned an entirely different Italy from the one desired by most nationalists. Italy was to be freed from the domination of the Pope and of Austria but not united in any real sense; and its independence was to be limited by the leadership of Piedmont and France (although who would be the dominant partner in this ruling partnership was left largely undecided).

In January 1859, an alliance was signed between France and Piedmont. Over the next four months, both states did everything they could to provoke Austria into declaring war. Efforts were made to foment insurrections in central Italy; volunteers were encouraged to present themselves for the fight against Austria; and both the king of Piedmont and Napoleon III made inflammatory speeches and remarks about the situation in Italy. Princess Clotilde's marriage to Prince Jerôme was announced. And although these plans for war suffered a temporary setback when Britain's attempt at mediation was accepted by the French, in the end Austria walked into the trap by threatening war if Piedmont did not immediately disarm. In April 1859, Piedmont refused and Austria declared war.

The war was short – just over two months – but it was decisive for the future of Italy. The combined armies of France and Piedmont narrowly defeated the Austrians at the battles of Magenta and Solferino, and in June Vittorio Emanuele and Napoleon III entered Milan to a triumphant welcome. Yet opposition at home, and the terrible violence of the two battles, led Napoleon to lose his nerve and in July he negotiated a separate peace with Franz Josef, the Austrian Emperor, at Villafranca. By the terms of this treaty, and to the fury of Cavour, Austria lost Lombardy but held on to Venice. Moreover, to save Austria's face, Lombardy was ceded first to France and only then to Piedmont, thus emphasising Piedmont's minor position in the European hierarchy of Great Powers. Finally, and despite a series of pro-Piedmontese revolts in the central Italian duchies and in the Legations, the status quo there (and with it Austrian and/or papal authority) was reaffirmed in the treaty.

Undeniable, nevertheless, was the defeat of Austria in northern Italy. During the months that followed Villafranca it proved impossible to restore the status quo, and the liberal governments which were set up in Tuscany and the Legations rejected their former rulers and sought a union with Piedmont. In March 1860, plebiscites were held in the central Italian states, and they resulted in an overwhelming vote in favour of Piedmontese rule. In the same month, Piedmont announced the annexation of Savoy and Nice to France.

So although the national and international outcry which arose after the cession of Savoy and Nice discredited Cavour (now back in power after a temporary withdrawal from politics), the result was largely in his favour. Piedmont had lost two border provinces and had failed to acquire Venice, but in return had gained control of Lombardy (the real prize) along with the considerable bonus of central Italy, defeating Austria and the Pope in the process. Besides, Napoleon III was bruised by the unpopularity of his Italian policy and began to withdraw from the peninsula. Piedmont was left in control of Italy.

Unification, 1860–70

At the moment of his greatest triumph, Cavour was forced to face his biggest challenge yet. The problems which he came to face were due to two unforeseen consequences of the war with Austria. First, as we have seen, the crisis of Austria in Italy was a calamity for Austria's Italian allies, and its defeat destabilised not just central Italy but the south of the peninsula as well. In particular, the loss of Austrian support had a devastating effect on the Kingdom of the Two Sicilies. Already reeling from financial problems and the death of the long-lived sovereign Ferdinando II, the Bourbon kingdom now lurched toward disaster. So, when a minor revolution broke out in Palermo and its provinces, the government prove unable to control it. Second, the vacuum left by the Austrians benefited not just Piedmont and the moderates, but their opponents too; and the months before and following the war were marked by an upsurge in unitarian nationalism. Democratic agitation in favour of continuing the war against Austria, and extending it to the Papal States, was led by Giuseppe Garibaldi, the most visible and popular symbol of the Italian Risorgimento. Until spring 1860, Cavour managed to hold back the twin tides of nationalism and revolution. But in the course of the spring, all this was to change.

In the war of 1859, Garibaldi had fought with Piedmont against Austria. A Mazzinian nationalist turned supporter of moderate liberalism in the hope of achieving unification, he was like most nationalists disillusioned by the peace of Villafranca and turned against Cavour in its aftermath. Devastated by the news that Cavour had ceded Nice, his home town, to France, he quickly recovered his revolutionary roots. It was in Sicily, where the news of revolution was being talked up by Mazzinian supporters in the island, that Garibaldi saw some hope, so he set sail from Genoa in early May, with about a thousand volunteers, to overthrow the Bourbon kingdom and unite the South with the rest of Italy. The expedition of the 'Thousand' was proclaimed in the name of Italy and the king of Piedmont ('*Italia e Vittorio Emanuele*'), but there was little doubt about Garibaldi's real intentions. These were to challenge Cavour, overturn the Italian settlement and, if successful in the South, march on Rome, take the city from the Pope and make it the capital of a democratic Italy.

The results exceeded all expectations. In less than six months, with apparent ease, Garibaldi defeated the Bourbon army, first in Sicily and then on the mainland, and overthrew the Bourbon kingdom. He put together a substantial (c.20,000 strong) volunteer army, made up largely of men from northern and central Italy but including some foreign enthusiasts as well; and he proclaimed himself dictator and reorganised the government, with an administration and police force modelled on the Piedmontese system, and introduced a number of far-reaching social reforms. Above all, his conquest of the South gave the democrats a solid basis of power. When, in September 1860, he entered Naples by train to a triumphant welcome it was to find the capital already abandoned by the Bourbon royal family, who had fled to their fortress in Capua a few days before. In October, Garibaldi defeated the Bourbon army on the Volturno river, thereby opening the road to Rome.

Few political leaders have captured the public imagination quite like Garibaldi. Still, the global enthusiasm that greeted his conquest of the Two Sicilies was not shared by the Piedmontese government. Horrified by the implications of Garibaldi's success for Cavour's design for Italy, whether this was through a resurgence of Mazzinianism or the provocation of French intervention to protect the Pope, Cavour determined to stop Garibaldi taking Rome. For that reason, in September 1860, he sent the Piedmontese army into and through the Papal States to meet Garibaldi north of Naples. The Piedmontese first defeated the papal forces at Castelfidardo, and took control of Umbria and the Marche, and in October the royal army, led by the king, met with Garibaldi's volunteer forces in a chilly encounter at Teano. Shortly before, amid growing problems of law and order and peasant violence over land, plebiscites held in the southern mainland and Sicily had voted in favour of annexation by Piedmont. In November, Garibaldi handed power over to Piedmont and left Naples for his island home on Caprera. The following year, in February, Italy was formally united, with Vittorio Emanuele II of Piedmont as its first king and Turin as its capital city.

Map 1.3   The Unification of Italy, 1859–70

From Lucy Riall, *Garibaldi: Invention of a Hero*, Yale University Press, 2007.

The years of the Risorgimento, and the events of Italian unification, are among the most mythologised in modern history, and they are also politically controversial. Behind the myth and the controversies lies the ambivalent nature of what happened in 1859–60. Garibaldi's greatest success ended in his own defeat; and the union of North and South took place in an atmosphere of distrust, disappointment and popular disorder. Italy was united with Venice still under Austria, and the Pope in Rome protected by a French garrison. Only in 1866, after a disastrous war with Austria, did Italy gain control of Venice; for Rome, the government had to wait another four years before Napoleon III withdrew his troops. And although Rome became the capital of Italy in 1870, Pope Pius IX maintained an implacable opposition to the new 'usurper' state, proclaiming himself (and his successors) a 'prisoner of the Vatican' and ordering loyal Catholics not to participate in Italian politics.

The problems of 'post-Risorgimento' Italy are discussed in chapter seven. But the central ironies of Italian unification are clear from this narrative of events. The main architects of unity, the Piedmontese moderate liberals, had no interest in the edifice. Those who had fought long and hard for its construction – Mazzini, Garibaldi, the democratic movement as a whole – had little part in the final result. The sense of difference and decline relative to European neighbours, which had driven successive attempts at reform and revolution in Italy since the mid-eighteenth century, was not reversed by the wars of 1859–60 with their dependence on France, the failure to reach Venice and Rome and the collapse of the Two Sicilies. The position of the people, also a thorn in the side of Italian reformers and revolutionaries from the Enlightenment onwards, was not altered by unification. Nor, for the most part, did the poor want or welcome these events.

Unification, so often celebrated as the culmination of Italy's struggle for freedom and unity, was in fact a contingent response to a grave and much longer-term political and social crisis. Events between 1848 and 1860 had simply made more visible the deep social and political divisions which had long destabilised the Italian peninsula, and these had at last exploded in 1859–60 into a bitter, and in many ways unresolved, struggle for power. The successors of Cavour, Garibaldi and Mazzini were to tussle with the

2

The Risorgimento and the History of Italy

Birth of a nation

In Italian history, as in Italian politics, the Risorgimento has played a central role. Much like the French Revolution, from which it drew part of its impetus, the Risorgimento is thought to be a turning-point for Italy, the start of its present history and the source of its shared identity. Through the Risorgimento, Italy gains its 'founding fathers' (Garibaldi, Mazzini, Vittorio Emanuele II, Cavour) and its main geographical boundaries. Most of all, the Risorgimento marks the emergence of Italy as a nation. With it, Italy is 'revived' and 'resurrected' (*risorta*); it acquires a new sense of itself, a fresh set of political ideals (liberalism, republicanism, nationalism) and a modern, nation-state.

This interpretation can certainly be challenged, as we will see. However, its significance in shaping our view of Italy's past is undeniable. Indeed, the concept of 'Risorgimento' has structured our knowledge of Italian history in several ways. First, Risorgimento denotes a period: traditionally 1815–60, although many historians now trace the beginnings of the period to the reforms of the late eighteenth century, and extend its conclusion to the seizure of Rome from the Pope in 1870 and the rise to power of the Historic Left government in 1876. Risorgimento also describes a process of modernisation. It encompasses a whole series of changes which took place in this period: the breakdown of traditional rural society and the birth of modern, urban life; the transition from a feudal to a capitalist economy; the crisis of the nobility and the rise of the middle classes; the replacement of local or regional identities by a single national culture; and the collapse of the old regime and the creation of a nation-state based on a parliamentary system of government.

Now, such complex transformations – sometimes happening quite rapidly, sometimes coming more slowly – are common to much of Europe in the same period, and Italy was deeply affected by events and trends emerging elsewhere. So our focus on Italy should not allow us to lose sight of what was happening in Europe. Just as the impact of the French Revolution and Napoleon were felt across the continent, so were the upheavals caused by population increase, migration to the cities and the commercialisation of agriculture. The growth of the middle classes took place unevenly, but it was still a Europe-wide phenomenon, which altered British, German, French and other European societies as much as, if not more than, Italy. Throughout Europe, the steady improvement in communications and the growth of state power began to break down the isolation of local communities and local identities, and in their place developed an idea of identity based on the nation and social networks of a national and transnational nature. Here too, Italy was part of a European movement. Everywhere, moreover, these changes produced disruption, displacement, disaffection and disorder.

Hence, none of the processes of change, and of resistance to change, which I will consider in this book were unique to Italy. Perhaps only in Italy, however, was such a systematic attempt made to harness and reinterpret them as a moment of 'revival' and 'resurrection' (the literal meaning of *risorgimento*). Arguably, it was also in Italy that the demand for 'resurrection' was linked most clearly to a liberal, opposition movement of political nationalism, and it was here that the nationalist movement captured public emotions and enthusiasm in an especially spectacular fashion. The strong sense of Italian distinctiveness was sometimes called 'primacy' (or Italy's civil, religious and political leadership of Europe) and the Risorgimento, by changing the way Italy was governed, was meant to recapture this pre-eminence for Italians. Risorgimento, in other words, describes a movement of political opposition, and it was used by Italian nationalists to promote and identify themselves. This political meaning is perhaps the most typical one, and the one most commonly used by historians to refer to the political struggles and events of the period.

A third way in which the Risorgimento has influenced our understanding of Italy's recent past is through the writing of history itself. Risorgimento (revival, resurrection) conveys a great deal: it describes the past and present, as well as the future. The term offers a quasi-religious promise of a better future, to be built on the memory of a more glorious past; but the term also implies a negative judgement on the present, and on those responsible for it. Italy, in the words of the romantic writer Ugo Foscolo, was a 'prostituted land' left with nothing 'except memory'.[1] In order to make convincing their political vision of the future, opposition leaders – men like Mazzini, Gioberti and (even) Cavour – relied on a heroic past of independence, unity and 'primacy' which validated their political demands, and they also referred to a squalid present of foreign oppression, internal divisions and defeat in order to belittle their ruling governments. Essentially, as a view of history, Risorgimento worked as a rhetorical device to promote Italian nationalist demands. The same view prevailed after unification, when it was reworked to interpret the recent past. Italy's new rulers professed to have fulfilled the Risorgimento, to have 'resurrected' the nation, while those they had defeated – notably, the Mazzinians – condemned its betrayal. In effect, the partisan struggles of Risorgimento involved the politicization of history, where all sides sought not just to hold on to the future but also to claim and master the past.

Again, Italy is not unique. Nationalists in both Germany and France sought out and relied on a 'foundation story' for the purposes of self-legitimation. As in Italy, references to their national past were sometimes fabrications, intended simply to lend plausibility to their political demands. Equally, debates about recent history were deeply politicised across Europe. In France, historians of the Revolution took sides for and against. After unification in Germany, nationalist historians rewrote the recent past, simplifying and distorting it to justify what had come about. In Germany as in Italy, politicians and historians worked together to create a heroic narrative of events which would make nation-state creation seem the inevitable, and morally correct, outcome of what was, in reality, a political struggle for power.[2]

What sets Italy apart is, once more, the idea of Risorgimento: ironically, the word reflects, and bestows on Italy, a sense of national decline which is largely missing in other western European nationalist movements. Acceptance of the word and its assumptions dictates a number of politically loaded questions, which are only thinly disguised as historical problems. For example: when did Italy start to decline? Above all: who and what is to blame for Italy's decay? How can its weakness be cured and who is able to do this? Has the decline really been reversed? The point is that the opposition politics of Risorgimento, by using Italy's celebrated past to criticise its present, recast Italy as a problem; so the assertion of national identity was shaped not only by an idea of revival but also by the language of corruption and failure. In turn, so successful was this language as a technique for winning support and defaming opponents that it became an accepted part of political and historical debate from the Risorgimento onwards. 'The Italy which we represent today . . . is a living lie', Mazzini wrote after his defeat at the hands of Cavour and the moderate liberals, 'this is just the ghost of Italy.'[3] Italy's past could always be rewritten to become better than its present; Italy could always be compared unfavourably to itself.

Equally, as both historians and politicians during the Risorgimento and thereafter soon discovered, history could not always be relied upon to justify nationalist demands. Calls for Italian unity were, if anything, undermined by recourse to the past: ancient Rome was glorious but was characterised by civil war and factionalism (the Republic), or by repression and decadence (the Empire). The medieval age of communal independence was heroic, but was also a period of political fragmentation and civil conflict. Particular episodes, such as the oath of Pontida (1167) and the Sicilian Vespers (1282) could be celebrated as moments of Italian solidarity (Pontida) and rebellion (the Vespers), but Pontida pointed equally to the importance of papal support for the idea of Italy while the Vespers evoked a deep fear of popular violence.[4] So, as a political weapon, history often proved too malleable for comfort, and it provided a somewhat fragile basis for the construction of a national foundation story in Italy.

All these meanings of Risorgimento: Risorgimento as a process of structural change and modernisation, Risorgimento as a political movement, and Risorgimento as an interpretation of history are considered in this book. By separating these three meanings, I aim to explain their effect on each other, and to understand how they came together to form a single narrative of national rebirth. How, for example, did nationalists interpret the structural changes affecting Italy in the early nineteenth century and how did they use history to press home their political demands? How did these changes constrain, condition or assist the nationalists in their programme? How have historians engaged with, distanced themselves from and/or otherwise sought to deal with the narrative of Risorgimento, with its attendant images of greatness, failure, decline and resurrection?

In the rest of this chapter, I look specifically at historical interpretations of the Risorgimento, and at some of the main debates about its character and achievements which have divided historians of Italy. I consider first the dispute among liberal and Marxist historians over the relationship between the Risorgimento and fascism, and how it produced a set of standards against which Italy was judged negatively. I then analyse 'revisionist' attempts, made during the 1980s, to challenge these negative judgements and to establish new models for investigating the social, economic and political transformations of the period. Finally, I analyse the importance of the 'new cultural history' for the study of the Risorgimento. My purpose is to disentangle the politics of the Risorgimento from the Risorgimento as history, and to assess the usefulness of the concept for our understanding of change in nineteenth-century Italy.

Liberal and Marxist interpretations

Contemporary attempts to investigate the history of the Risorgimento date back to fascism and its aftermath. In part, this was due to the fascist regime's interest in the period. Led by the philosopher Giovanni Gentile, it reaffirmed the importance of the Risorgimento as the founding event of the nation, and as a process of renewal that reached its true fulfilment in fascist totalitarianism.[5] Also under fascism, vast collections of original documents – letters, diaries and official correspondence – relating to the period and its protagonists were assembled and placed in archives. Once opened to the public after the Second World War, these primary sources were to shed new light on the political struggles of the Risorgimento.

With the collapse of the regime and the end of the Second World War, Gentile's interpretation of the Risorgimento as precursor to fascism was abandoned. What remained was a sense of the importance of the Risorgimento to everything that came after. Thus, the task that fell to historians who opposed fascism was how to explain what had gone wrong: how to explain the utter collapse of liberal Italy in 1922, only sixty years after the nation's 'resurrection' had been proclaimed at the moment of unification. Two conflicting accounts emerged: one first outlined by the liberal philosopher Benedetto Croce in 1928, the other written during the fascist period by the imprisoned Marxist activist Antonio Gramsci, but published only in 1949.[6]

Croce's primary aim was to defend the achievements of Italian liberalism. Those who had made Italy in 1860 were, in his words, 'a spiritual aristocracy of upright and loyal gentlemen'.[7] They were men of a noble, honest and self-sacrificing character. Any problems that developed in liberal Italy after national unification had little to do with these men; Italy's weaknesses were instead due to decisions taken much later and to the huge political, financial and diplomatic difficulties that the new nation faced. Moreover, despite these difficulties Italy's leaders had always maintained their commitment to the liberal parliamentary system until the disaster of the First World War. Croce insisted that it was only the war that destroyed liberalism and made the rise of fascism possible. He denied any causal connection between Italian liberalism and Italian fascism: fascism was a historical 'parenthesis', an aberration produced by the war. The political ideals of fascism, in particular its commitment to a one-party state, were the 'antithesis' of liberalism.

Although influenced by Croce's idealist philosophy, Gramsci opposed his political and historical arguments. Gramsci argued instead that there was something profoundly wrong with Italian liberalism, and he drew a series of links between fascism and liberalism, tracing both back to the tensions generated by class struggle in the Risorgimento. He depicted the Risorgimento as a 'passive revolution', or as a 'revolution without a revolution'. The moderate liberals had out-manoeuvred the democrats, and had come to power by defeating the revolution and reaching a compromise with the old 'feudal' regime. They claimed to have rebuilt Italy, but the truth was that they had sacrificed real social and political change to their own narrow class interests. The price of their compromise with the old regime was a permanent breach between the Italian state and Italian civil society, characterised by chronic political instability and endemic social disorder. Fascism, Gramsci argued, was the direct product of this situation. It was an attempt by a weak bourgeoisie to recast a political system which had definitively collapsed in 1919, and to use coercion to counter class unrest and, specifically, to defeat the socialist revolution which threatened in the same period.

Gramsci's prison dialogue with Croce set up a series of oppositions that dominated historical research on the Risorgimento, and which reflected post-war politics, specifically the struggle between right and left in Italy after 1945. The Crocean (or right-wing, liberal) depiction of political progress and harmony was challenged by a Gramscian (or left-wing, Marxist) one which emphasised social conflict. On the one hand, liberal historians proposed a narrative made up of glorious moments, heroic action and concrete achievement; Marxists, on the other, stressed class repression, internal divisions and political defeat. They drew attention to the potential for revolutionary change in the Risorgimento, to the differences between moderates and democrats, and to the failure of revolution and its dire consequences for the political and economic development of Italy. By contrast, liberal historians pointed to the barriers to progress, and to the skill with which they had been overcome: Cavour's 'audacious' programme of reform without revolution was said to be without parallel in Europe.[8] It was the intellectual vigour of the moderate liberals which ensured their leadership over the more utopian democrats. Given Italy's dependence on foreign powers, its internal disunity, its reactionary rulers and its economic backwardness, liberal historians concluded that the scale of the moderate party's success was truly impressive.

Underlying these oppositions was a conflict of historical interpretation: between a liberal view of history as a movement of ideas and individuals, and a Marxist one which saw history as the process of class struggle. This difference is worth stressing because in other ways the two approaches shared many common concerns and assumptions. More precisely, both Marxist and liberal historians were driven by the need to explain the ultimate defeat of the Risorgimento, and to identify the causes of, and responsibility for, this disappointing outcome. In both accounts, modern Italy's divergence from a general middle-class, democratic European norm was assumed.

Liberal historians pointed to the problems of Italian society, to the slow development of the Italian economy, to cultural differences and to a weak foreign position, and defended what had been done, concluding that Italy's leaders could not have done any better. Marxists argued instead that the nationalists were too weak, too timid and too corrupt to make a revolution, and the end result – unification under moderate liberalism and monarchical Piedmont – frustrated the potential for social change, political reform and cultural revival in the nation. What had happened was the nationalist movement's fault. But whether the failure was Italy's or its leaders, both sides agreed on the underlying problems. These were the weakness of the middle classes, the backwardness of the economy, the lack of popular enthusiasm for the nation, the persistence of local identities and the repressive legacy of Italy's Restoration (or post-1815, old regime) states. For both, the social and economic transformations that should have taken place in the Risorgimento had not occurred, and in this respect the Risorgimento had not succeeded.

These explanations of liberal Italy's failure after 1860 rest on a view of the Risorgimento as a struggle between progress (whether represented by the moderate liberals, the democrats or the revolution itself) and reaction (the Restoration states, the backward economy and the archaic social structure). This interpretation was extremely influential. Outside Italy, scholars were less involved in the politics of history, and less obliged to take up a left- or right-wing position on the Risorgimento. Nevertheless, they too tended to assume that Italy was historically a failure, and they too found confirmation of failure in fascism and its collapse. At the beginning of the twentieth century, the Risorgimento had found its greatest champion in the British liberal historian, George Macaulay Trevelyan, who recast the events of unification as a morality tale: a struggle between good (the nationalists) and evil (the forces of reaction), with the triumph of progress in 1860.[9] But British enthusiasm for Italy changed during fascism and after 1945. During the 1950s, one historian – Denis Mack Smith – took brilliant advantage of the opening of new archives to reveal the rivalry and double-dealing which had accompanied, and indeed resulted in, Italian unification.[10] Thereafter, a tone of disillusion and condescension crept into many English language treatments of the Risorgimento and Italian leadership, and, until recently at least, it proved difficult to dislodge.

Cavour, in the words of the popular historian A. J. P. Taylor, 'did not care much about the unification of Italy'. The democrats 'had plenty of chances' but 'never made much' of them; and, he suggested, 'Italy has been kept going (so far as it goes at all) by hard-headed officials of Cavour's stamp.'[11] For many who looked at the Risorgimento with an eye to what came after, Italy's history between 1815 and 1870 became a story of broken promises and missed opportunities, which had given rise to a country of regret, corruption and thwarted ambition.

The end of the Risorgimento

After 1945, a combination of disappointed expectations and political divisions produced a set of historical standards for interpreting the Risorgimento. These identified bad leaders, economic backwardness and/or social stagnation as the causes of liberal failure. During the 1980s, however, these considerations began to change. In part, this change was generational: many of the protagonists in post-war debates reached retirement age at this time. A younger generation of historians, born after 1945, started to question many of the basic assumptions of Risorgimento historiography. In the course of the 1980s, moreover, the nineteenth-century faith in liberty and progress lost what remained of its relevance, the patriotism of the Risorgimento seemed increasingly outmoded and misguided, and the personal links of empathy and memory which had tied historians of previous generations to the century of their fathers disappeared.[12] One historian complained that the Risorgimento had held the nineteenth century 'hostage', by dominating the historical agenda and blocking other avenues of enquiry.[13]

The arrival of the 'new social history' during the 1970s and '80s made perhaps the most significant difference to historical research in Italy. Although its original impulse was Marxist, the new social history soon outgrew these roots (if not its left-wing sympathies), and its horizons expanded to take in an interest in work, women and wealth, and a concern with poverty, policing and rural life. It came to shake all the certainties of research into the history of the Risorgimento. Historians started to question the idea of modernisation, implicit in both the Marxist concept of revolution as well as in the liberal concept of progress, and many switched their attention to other periods: to the moment of rapid industrialisation in the late nineteenth century or to fascism and its aftermath. Influenced by other disciplines such as anthropology, some historians began to study much smaller units; regions, communities and families became a main focus of research. Historical research in Italy thus came to involve a great plurality where neither the importance of the Risorgimento nor the inevitability of the nation-state was taken for granted. National unification acquired a different significance as a partial solution to a specific set of political problems, rather than as a general break (however flawed in practice) with a more traditional past.

During the late 1980s and 1990s, a process of historical 'revision' got underway, which began to challenge the periodisation, methodologies, subjects and interpretations of both the Marxist and liberal schools. There were two especially innovative areas of research, both of which have important implications for our understanding of the Risorgimento. First, historians began to reconsider the issue of class, and to suggest that much closer attention be paid

to the successes of the Italian middle classes and the diverse forms
of middle-class identity. Life in the countryside, land-ownership,
reliance on family wealth and support, all of these characteristics
were once felt to be proof of the backwardness of the Italian bourgeoisie; but, with further investigation, this behaviour was found to
be part of a rational, self-interested and winning strategy for acquiring wealth and social status.[14]

Along with a more positive view of the middle classes, a different picture of Italy's Restoration states emerged. The most obvious
beneficiary was the Austrian administration of Lombardy and
Venetia, once a symbol of reactionary and oppressive misgovern-
ment. From the early 1980s, extensive new research pointed to the
relative responsiveness of Vienna and Austrian administrators to
local demands and to the role played by government in overseeing
rapid economic growth in this region.[15] The part played by King
Carlo Alberto of Piedmont (1831–49) in bringing about political
and economic reform, and thus his responsibility for the liberal
transformation that followed in the 1850s, was also stressed.[16]
Instead of being an attempt to return to the old regime after 1815,
the Restoration states were recast by historians as harbingers of
political change, at once more liberal and more efficient than had
previously been thought.

I will explore the implications of this new research in more detail
in chapters three, four and five of this book. One of the general
effects of new research was to undermine the sense of failure and
difference which had long attached itself to Italy and the
Risorgimento. In fact, historical revisionism in Italy was paralleled
by similar challenges and debates in France, Germany and the
English-speaking world. For example, Marxist interpretations of
German liberalism came under attack for their reliance on models
of political and economic development that were artificially
constructed from the English and French experiences. Revisions in
both French revolutionary and British liberal history confirmed
that no single model of liberalism and capitalism had ever existed.
Moreover, much more emphasis came to be placed on historical
continuity rather than change, and on the ways in which the old
regime everywhere in Europe survived well into the twentieth
century.[17] Thus, the capacity of the old nobility to adapt to capi-

talism, and the relative weakness of the middle classes, seemed no longer to be peculiar to Italy, but a feature of all European societies in this period. Italy had not strayed from any set path to modernisation, since no such path existed. It seemed increasingly that Italy's failure to modernise was a problem invented by its historians, influenced by artificial models of political and economic development as well as by the drastic experiences of fascism and war.

Where did the disintegration of these well-established categories leave historians of the Risorgimento? One result was to free historians to seek new narratives and new models for interpreting the society and politics of nineteenth-century Italy. Many came to study state formation, that is, the growth of central government and the establishment of modern bureaucracies and armies, and the complex relations between state and society; and state formation was increasingly considered the key to understanding the dynamics of change in the peninsula. This interest in the state involved a broadening of chronological focus – away from just the Risorgimento, and towards the eighteenth and twentieth centuries – as well as a focus on political and administrative institutions and on relations between centre and periphery. In effect, this also shifted historical attention away from nationalist revolutionaries and towards the rulers and servants of the Restoration states, who were usually not nationalists at all. Moreover, state formation was treated as a process independent of changes in society and the economy; it was seen as something entirely autonomous and with a logic of its own, driven by forces (the political and bureaucratic elites) inside the state. This conceptualisation of state formation as a development separate from society owes more to Max Weber than to Karl Marx, and it challenged the hitherto established equation of industry and capitalism with the rise of liberal democracy.

As we will see, this approach to Risorgimento history is extremely valuable, and has greatly enhanced our appreciation of the diverse ways modernisation affected the Italian peninsula. The problem is what was left out. Elites, middle class and noble, became the centre of research; it was they who were responsible for state formation, so the ordinary people, peasants and proletariat, who had been the original subject of the 'new social history', seemed often irrelevant. The role of religion and the Church was almost entirely forgotten. The emphasis on structural change – on state, economy and society – ignored the role of political ideas and political struggle in bringing about change. Above all perhaps, the idea of the nation, and of the Italian Risorgimento, faded from view. Work on Risorgimento politics stagnated. The term's political meaning, its importance as a tool of opposition and a vision of belonging, and the need to explain the rise and popularity of the nation as a political idea and its use in the struggle for power – all this was largely sidelined.

Revisionist historians of the Risorgimento rightly rejected both Marxist ideas of class struggle and liberal notions of freedom and progress because these failed to provide adequate explanations for what had happened in Italy between the arrival of Napoleon and the formation of the nation-state. Yet they did not develop an alternative means of studying and understanding political struggle. In fact, the emphasis on state formation and the industrious middle classes tended to overlook the reality of conflict and crisis in nineteenth-century Italy. Nationalism was ignored rather than explained. But by neglecting political struggle and the rise of nationalism, historians proved unable to provide an answer to what remained, for better or worse, a fundamental question: why did national unification happen at all?

Risorgimento revived?

In the last few years, historians of Italian culture have forced us to confront this question once again, and in particular they have reopened and relaunched the debate on the nature and achievements of Italian nationalism. Starting with the publication of Alberto Banti's *L'idea della nazione* in 2000, something of a new school of historical research has been established which focuses on the creation and diffusion of an idea of Italy through literature, music and art.[18] A great deal of new research follows the approach outlined by Banti (which I discuss in chapter 6) and it concentrates on a close analysis of what he calls the 'national-patriotic discourse' of Risorgimento Italy. Romanticism, and the impact of romantic sensibilities on nationalist ideas and practices, has emerged as an important new area of research. Other complementary themes have also emerged, and these link the analysis of nationalism to broader changes in culture, society and politics.

For example, a notable re-evaluation of nineteenth-century painting and music has occurred, alongside a new assessment of the Italian literary scene (an analysis of writers, publishers and readers, and the whole sphere of cultural production).[19] Research into political and associational networks, and in the history of ideas, has revealed the extent to which Risorgimento nationalists were linked to a wider, liberal and international, public.[20] Historians have used a gender analysis to examine Italian nationalism, and have offered us new insights into the relationship between public and private in nineteenth-century Italy.[21] Others have focused on the creation of symbols of Italy and 'Italian-ness' before and after unification, and on the changing public response to them.[22]

Taken together, this research has changed our conception of the Risorgimento. It involves another shift of focus: away from social and economic change and state formation, and back again to the idea of the nation and Italian nationalism. However, this shift has not involved a return to the old debates of post-war Italy. The class struggles which preoccupied Marxist historians in the 1950s and 60s have been discarded, but so too, largely, has the interest in high politics and political struggle which was more characteristic of the liberal approach. Now culture is the dominant motif, and it is in written and visual culture that historians look for evidence of change, rebellion and 'Risorgimento'. More important than politics itself is the experience and memory of political action; and at this time historians are most interested in how people lived the Risorgimento, how they took part in, felt about and described these activities, and how they remembered what they had done. On this basis, a much more optimistic assessment of the achievements and significance of the Risorgimento has emerged.

Risorgimento explained

This volume is intended as a guide to the different ways in which the Risorgimento has been lived, described and understood. I take a broadly thematic rather than a strictly chronological approach, although the narrative of events provided in chapter one guides many of the questions asked elsewhere in the book. The bibliography at the end of the book offers suggestions for further study.

While I agree with revisionist historians who suggest that the idea of 'Risorgimento' has blinded us to other events and processes taking place in the Italian peninsula at this time, I also argue that we need to understand and seek to explain the nation: that is, we need to clarify the force and appeal of Italian nationalism as well as the unexpected events of Italian unification. Moreover, what makes the Risorgimento interesting is precisely the connections and the disparities between economic, social, political and cultural change, and the ways in which these processes were experienced differently in the various parts of the peninsula. So, any analysis of events in this period needs to incorporate the interaction between these very diverse factors. The Risorgimento also provides us with some fascinating examples of how so many people, rich and poor, responded to social and political change. Thus, we should consider how a new idea of Italy emerged as a means of explaining and controlling these changes, why nationalism became popular among certain sections of the population (but not among others) and whether it ever worked as a solution to Italy's problems.

In the chapters that follow, I look at government, society and the economy in the period of the Restoration (1815 to 1860). Chapter 3 assesses the attempts of Restoration rulers to establish stable regimes in the Italian peninsula; chapters 4 and 5 analyse the evidence for social change and economic development in Restoration Italy. In these chapters, I focus in particular on the contribution of 'revisionist' historians to enriching our understanding of the process of modernisation in Italy, and I consider the achievements and problems of this perspective. I argue that the overall results of this research demonstrate the unplanned character of Italian unification and tend to downplay the importance of Risorgimento and Italian nationalism.

Yet in the absence of any inexorable drive towards the nation, we need a new explanation of the Risorgimento and the unification of Italy. In chapter 6, I analyse the role of culture in the growth of an idea of Italy. I suggest that research into culture leads to a different

As a result of the defeat of Austria in 1859 and the victory of the liberal-national movement, the liberal critique of Restoration government became the official history of the Risorgimento. Even in the Marxist analyses that became popular in the 1950s and 1960s, this liberal interpretation of the Risorgimento in terms of a struggle between progress and reaction had great force. The attraction lay in how much this simple dichotomy could explain: the growth of a liberal movement could be linked to the emergence of a capitalist economy and the rise of industrial society, while the reactionary policies of Restoration governments could be attributed to the resistance of feudal or pre-capitalist elements to a change in economic production. In turn, the establishment of a united Italy seemed to be part of a more general epoch of bourgeois progress in Europe, an epoch that produced a liberal political structure which was more appropriate to the needs of capitalism and industrial society.

The association of the Risorgimento with progress and improvement meant that Restoration government was rarely given much attention. If progress was the basis of Risorgimento, then why bother with those who clung to the past? So, liberal opinion depicted Restoration Italy as dominated by a conservative alliance of 'throne and altar' which sustained clerical privileges and religious corruption, and historians took this alliance for granted. Similarly, political opposition in the South before and after unification presented the Bourbon kingdom as the epitome of reaction, and this example was accepted uncritically by historians. The repression of popular unrest and the establishment of surveillance networks against the revolutionary threat in post-1815 Italy was, in the same way, understood simply as proof of reactionary attitudes and regressive tendencies, and little effort was made to analyse the political struggles which lay behind these policies.

Risorgimento liberals also criticised the economic policies of the Restoration regimes. In particular, they complained about the maintenance of protectionist barriers against foreign goods and the failure to improve the economic infrastructure. Historians too have seen these policies as crucial in explaining the wider unpopularity of Restoration government. In Lombardy-Venetia, for example, it was argued in liberal circles that the protectionist policies of the Austrian Empire benefited Austria at the expense of local interests.

High taxation was also considered to help the imperial treasury in Vienna by draining Lombardy-Venetia of its economic resources. Such accusations were repeated in historical research: these wealthy Italian provinces (especially Lombardy) were the 'milch cow' of the Austrian Empire, victims of Austrian greed and European indifference.[3] Echoing liberal and nationalist rhetoric, moreover, the pursuit of these policies was assumed, not investigated, and was linked to the growth of political opposition after 1815.

More recent revisionist studies of Restoration Italy have rejected this approach. Specifically, new research has led historians to deny the all-purpose association of Restoration with reaction, and to question whether these governments were ever as backward-looking as assumed. Since the 1980s, a growing scepticism about progress and modernity has also meant that the opposition between progress and reaction seems unjustified and unworkable. As one historian, Marino Berengo, pointed out, accounts of Austrian misrule in Lombardy-Venetia were more a 'black myth' of nationalist writing than the product of serious historical analysis.[4] This challenge to the negative assumptions of 'reaction' has formed the basis for a new research agenda.

In this chapter, I take the revisionist account of the Italian Restoration as my starting point. Instead of a monolithic system of reactionary government, we will find a great variety of regimes, some progressive and some much more conservative. Furthermore, governments changed and, indeed, adapted to changing times and rulers. Most obviously, Piedmont was among the most reactionary of states immediately after 1815, but forty years later, after two revolutions and three kings, became by far the most liberal. Equally, there was a great variety of responses to the Restoration. The return of the old regimes was often widely welcomed, and, where it was not, opposition was due as much to resistance to reform (and 'progress') as it was to any unfulfilled desire for change. It is clear that modernisation, and the problems associated with it, did not stop with the fall of Napoleon. Administrative reform often continued, centralisation remained and the tensions between monarch and nobility, Church and state, and state and society persisted, whether or not the old regime was fully restored. If a comparative perspective is adopted, finally, neither the prob-

lems nor the repressive policies of Restoration Italy seem so different from those experienced and pursued in Germany and France,
or even in Great Britain. So Restoration Italy's problems no longer
seem peculiar to Italy, or to derive necessarily from political backwardness.

The effect of these challenges to historical orthodoxy is to pose
a new set of questions about the Risorgimento and Italian unification. For example, if the governments of Restoration Italy were
neither reactionary nor unusually repressive, how do we explain
the growth of liberalism and nationalism? If they were not especially unpopular, inefficient or repressive, why did they ultimately
collapse? It is by creating these uncertainties, as we shall see, that
revisionist research has dissolved the opposition between
Restoration reaction and Risorgimento progress and, in the process,
has cast doubt on the causes and inevitability of national unification.

Administrative monarchy

Despite the reactionary reputation of Restoration Italy, determined
attempts to 'turn the clock back' to before the French Revolution
were confined to a few rulers at specific times. The most complete
experiments were carried out by King Vittorio Emanuele I of
Piedmont and Duke Francesco IV of Modena in the immediate
Restoration period, and by the Papacy between 1823 and 1846.

The government of Piedmont after 1814 is perhaps the most
striking example of reaction at work. Following his return from
exile, the king abolished all Napoleonic legislation and reinstated
the legislation of the old regime with one single decree. Duke
Francesco IV took similar measures in Modena. In both these states,
a purge of the administrative and judicial personnel, whose
numbers had been expanded in the Napoleonic period to include
men of the middle classes, was also carried out. All the officials who
had served in the Napoleonic Kingdom of Italy were dismissed in
Modena, and the Duke proceeded to fill the upper echelons of his
bureaucracy with members of the old nobility. In Piedmont, hered-
itary privilege replaced the Napoleonic criteria of talent and train-

ing as the means of accession and promotion to the higher ranks of the bureaucracy. Pre-Napoleonic office holders were recalled to their posts, using the Savoy court almanac of 1798 as the guide. If an official had died in the interim, he was replaced by his son. The Piedmontese army, a stronghold of Napoleonic 'new men', was also purged.[5]

The economic and social policies pursued by Vittorio Emanuele I's government were also quite reactionary: internal and external barriers to trade were erected, old trade corporations and guilds were revived and feudal structures such as primogeniture and *fedecommesso* (property trusts) were reintroduced. The old judicial system, with its noble privileges and special jurisdictions, replaced the Napoleonic codes. The political, as well as the religious, union of throne and altar was reaffirmed. In both these states, not just the French Revolution but also the principles of eighteenth-century Enlightenment were rejected and reversed. Control of education was handed back to the Church, and the return of the Jesuits was welcomed in both Piedmont and Modena. Religious intolerance was affirmed when the laws against Jews, restricting their property rights and confining them to ghettos, were also reinstated.

Another attempt to return to the old regime was made in the Papal States after the election to Pope of the arch-reactionary Leo XII in 1823. Leo XII, and his successors Pius VIII and Gregory XVI, represented the reactionary group known as the 'zealots'. During the reign of these Popes, the Church's hold over the bureaucracy, education and culture was tightened. Religious persecution was intensified. A papal encyclical in 1824 condemned all forms of tolerance (*tollerantismo*). Strict censorship was imposed via the Papal Inquisition, and any sign of political opposition was repressed with force.[6]

It is significant, however, that where reactionaries succeeded in determining the direction of policy, their efforts to restore the old regime generally ended in failure. Political instability, rather than the return to order hoped for in 1815, was the more common outcome. With the exception of 1848–49, when revolutionary disturbances occurred across Italy, revolutions tended to occur precisely in those states (Piedmont, Modena, the Papal States) where the most reactionary policies had been pursued. In this most basic way, reaction was not a success. Its effect was to exacerbate, rather than resolve, the tensions between state and society, and it did little to control or alleviate the problems caused by social and economic change.

It is also revealing that reaction proved counter-productive not only (or even primarily) because of the extent of opposition but also because the dismantling of Napoleonic political structures was virtually self-defeating. Napoleonic administration was designed to guarantee centralised direction and efficient government, an aim which many eighteenth-century Italian monarchs had shared but failed to achieve. By abolishing this system, reactionary governments destroyed a vital instrument of executive power and political control, and attempted to replace it with an older, less potent structure which had long ago ceased to function properly. In purging the army and bureaucracy, they deprived these institutions of their most able men. The dismissal or demotion of Napoleonic officials and army officers also created considerable discontent and led to political agitation, thus further endangering political stability.

Not surprisingly, elsewhere in Italy, and perhaps most markedly in the Austrian kingdom of Lombardy-Venetia, an attempt was made to reconcile absolutist political structures with the need for political innovation. This policy of 'amalgamation' was actively encouraged by the Austrian Chancellor Prince Metternich who, despite his reputation for conservatism, consistently sought to prevent reactionaries from coming to power in Italy. Amalgamation consisted of an attempt to combine the eighteenth-century principles of reforming or 'enlightened' absolutism with the administrative and political modernisation of the Napoleonic era. The plan was to create what historians, borrowing a term from early-modern France, call 'administrative monarchies'; and these administrative monarchies were based on the principle that an efficient, modern bureaucracy and a centralised administration were crucial to the establishment of absolutism: in short, that modernisation and the maintenance of absolute authority were not incompatible. Many Restoration governments accepted that economic growth was equally essential to political stability.

So, after a brief period of reaction during the Restoration of 1814–15, a policy of amalgamation was pursued by Cardinal

Consalvi in the Papal States (before the accession of Leo XII in 1823), and by the government ministers Vittorio Fossombroni in Tuscany (where there was considerable continuity with eighteenth-century reforms) and Luigi de' Medici in the Two Sicilies. Encouraged by Metternich, all these ministers attempted to create more uniform and centralised administrations and to take account of revolutionary ideas and innovations. In these states, the personnel of the Napoleonic and old regime administrations was amalgamated in an effort to find the most capable and loyal officials. In Naples in 1815, the Austrian and British governments directly intervened to block the reactionary policies of the Principe di Canosa and to enforce de' Medici's policy of conciliation and reform. Consalvi made a strong (if failed) attempt to open up the papal bureaucracy to lay officials. Other areas of amalgamation included the judicial system and public education. Many states also embarked upon ambitious (if often unrealised) programmes of public works; and the governments of Lombardy-Venetia, Tuscany and the Two Sicilies intervened to encourage economic growth in specific regions.

These attempts at reform were not confined to the immediate period after the restoration of 1815. In fact, following the revolutionary upheavals of the early 1830s, Metternich again intervened in Italy: not just to help in the prevention and repression of political unrest but also in an effort to broaden support for Restoration government through what was called consultationary monarchy. First proposed through the Great Powers' 'Memorandum of 1831', which pressed for administrative and legal reforms in the Papal States, consultationary monarchy was based on the Austrian system of local government or congregations, which was already in force in Lombardy-Venetia, Tuscany and Parma.[7]

The consultationary system was another amalgam: this time a combination of the eighteenth-century Austrian model and the Napoleonic centralised structure. It was an attempt to modernise political absolutism through internal administrative reform. So Metternich proposed the establishment of a hierarchical system of communal, provincial and central councils which would have the task of presenting local demands and opinions to the central government, and which could include new, as well as more traditional, social and economic interests. The councils would perform a representative function and in this way, Metternich hoped, they would preclude the need for other representative institutions such as elections and parliaments, which he – like other European conservatives – associated with the chaos and violence of the French Revolution. These proposals met with some short-term success. In Piedmont and the Two Sicilies, state councils along the lines proposed by Metternich were established during the 1830s. Following the election of Pope Pius IX in 1846, a state council was established in Rome as well.

Outside Lombardy-Venetia, the two most important experiments in conservative reform along the lines proposed by Metternich took place in the Papal States after 1846, and in Piedmont during the reign of Carlo Alberto (1831–49). In the two years between 1846 and 1848, the new Pope Pius IX introduced major administrative changes, granted amnesties to political prisoners, dissolved the special commission in the Papal Legations and loosened the controls on the press. The anti-Jewish laws were also relaxed. A programme of public works was ordered, measures were taken to relieve a severe famine prevailing in parts of the Papal States and a customs union with Tuscany and Piedmont was concluded. These reforms created great excitement, especially in liberal-national circles where the possibility of papal support for their programme was given a huge welcome. Yet the pace of reform was too fast for Prince Metternich, who found the new Pope 'lacking in all practical sense'.[8]

In the once reactionary state of Piedmont, a longer and more concerted process of reform was also embarked upon after 1831. Once on the throne, King Carlo Alberto reversed the intransigent policies of his predecessors, and modernised and centralised the Piedmontese state along Napoleonic lines. The Napoleonic penal and civil codes were reintroduced; the central and local administrations were remodelled on the hierarchical French system of prefectures, sub-prefectures and communes; and the army was reorganised. Arguably, Carlo Alberto's financial, economic and educational reforms of the 1840s also began the process of change that was to transform the Piedmontese economy in the 1850s. A railway line was built by the state between Turin and Genoa, and Piedmont's high tariff barriers were reduced. Feudalism was abolished in Sardinia as part of a fairly substantial package of reforms

Figure 3.1   Pope Pius IX.
Library of Congress Prints and Photographs, Washington, DC, USA.

Pius IX was the first Pope to be photographed. His election as the 'liberal Pope' caused great excitement, which was rapidly disappointed as he proved to be a staunch conservative. However, his personal charm, shown clearly in this photograph, remained undiminished throughout his long reign.

designed to improve conditions in the island.[9] More generally, during the 1830s and early 1840s, his government made several (unsuccessful) attempts to establish an Italian customs union along the lines of the German *Zollverein* and to co-operate over the construction of an Italian railway network.

Such efforts to maintain a balance between the establishment of absolute authority and the need for reform or modernisation also extended to religion and the Church. Outside the Papal States, few of the Concordats signed between Restoration governments and the Church restored totally the Church's pre-revolutionary powers or sought to reverse the secularisation introduced by Napoleon. Indeed, we can perceive the first signs of the damaging split between Church and state in Italy in the changes introduced by Restoration governments, and not simply in the more openly secular policies of liberal Italy. After 1815, different regimes from Venice to Naples actually sought to contain and control the power of the clergy. Thus, the Restoration Concordats, however morally conservative and unpopular with liberals, actually confirmed the pre-eminent role of the state in civil society and the end of many clerical privileges. After 1815, control of censorship in Lombardy-Venetia and the Two Sicilies was exercised by the state, not by the Church. The 1818 Concordat with Naples abolished clerical immunities and the crown was allowed to nominate all bishops; and relations between the Bourbon state and the Church hierarchy remained difficult throughout the Restoration period.

The failure of reform

There is a clear distinction between the reactionary governments of rulers like Vittorio Emanuele I, Francesco IV and Leo XII, which sought to return to a quasi-feudal era before the reforms of the eighteenth century, and those administrations, best represented by conservative reformers such as Consalvi in the Papal States or de' Medici in the Two Sicilies, which attempted to amalgamate eighteenth-century and revolutionary reforms and create administrative monarchies based on a form of modernised absolutism. Differences also exist between both these models and the one adopted by

Fossombroni in the Grand Duchy of Tuscany, which built more directly on the traditions of eighteenth-century reform. These differences suggest there can be no single reason for the collapse of Restoration government in Italy. In particular, previous interpretations, which point to the persistence of a reactionary alliance with the Church, hostility to administrative modernisation and/or a reluctance to encourage economic growth, cannot explain why the various attempts at amalgamation and modernisation failed.

In reality, conservative reformers in the Restoration states were undermined, not by their resistance to change, but by their failure to establish an effective middle way between reaction and revolution. One symptom of this problem was the inability of conservative reformers to carry out an effective process of administrative reform. On the one hand, the old nobility expected a great deal from the Restoration. Along with the Church, they had remained loyal to the monarchy during revolution and exile, and wanted more power and positions of power in return for their support than their rulers were usually prepared to give. On the other hand, the 'new men' of the middle class were angered by their expulsion from the bureaucracy, and the restriction thereafter of high positions in the administration to members of the nobility.[10] Yet efforts made to mediate between middle-class and noble interests only compromised and isolated the central administration. In particular, the system of congregations satisfied neither one class nor the other.

Administrative reform, by offending both established and new interests, could create as many problems as it solved. These affected not only relations between social classes but also created tensions between central power and regional or local power-holders. It has long been recognised that resentment of central government in the provinces, and a profound dislike of the privileges and corruption of the Bourbon capital in Naples, lay behind the support given to revolution in the Two Sicilies in 1820.[11] The growth of liberal and republican opposition movements in the Papal Legations (against Rome), in Genoa (against Turin) and in Livorno (against Florence) can also be attributed to a desire for regional autonomy. Thus, regional resentments and administrative tensions between centre and periphery may have played a more important role in the growth of opposition movements than liberal sentiments and/or class interests. Moreover, these kinds of problems were probably accentuated by the post-1815 territorial settlement, which consolidated larger states. It is possible that the main cause of 'nationalist' unrest in Restoration Italy was not so much resentment at foreign or domestic oppression as it was dislike of territorial reorganisation and centralisation, which created new local and regional rivalries.[12]

So the drive to modernise, by exacerbating old tensions or creating new ones, could constrain and undermine the process of conservative reform. Sometimes local power-holders successfully resisted centralisation. For example, in rural Sicily and in parts of the Papal States, government attempts at economic reform and administrative modernisation were undermined by the collective opposition of the bourgeoisie and nobility. In the South, effective political power was retained by the local power-holders, who actually strengthened themselves *vis-à-vis* the central government by allying themselves with the middle class and by manipulating reforming legislation to their own personal advantage. Thus, despite persistent and significant conflicts within southern communities (which are discussed in the next chapter), the use of public power for private gain became a prominent feature of political and social life and frustrated central government improvements.[13]

All these factors suggest that reaction could be less unpopular than modernisation, and that central governments failed to achieve a balance between competing interests. This failure is evident in other areas too. For instance, Bourbon land reforms alienated the old nobility without satisfying the demands of the agrarian bourgeoisie. If liberals were offended by the levels of political surveillance, other groups were equally alarmed by the failure of many Restoration states to guarantee law and order, protect property or police the people effectively. In areas of frequent peasant unrest (the Southern and Sicilian *latifundia,* the Venetian plain) local power-holders tended to demand more, rather than less, repression. Yet central government responses to these demands were undermined by their lack of control on the ground: all over Italy, Restoration governments struggled to recruit loyal and trained personnel to act as police officers or to serve in local bureaucracies.

Administrative activity, the practical performance of central government decisions by its local representatives, plays a crucial role in explaining the chronic instability of the decades between 1815 and 1860. The lack of policy implementation, inefficient bureaucracies and bad policing, any number of financial crises – all of these problems may well have been more important in demoralising and isolating Restoration government than demands for liberal reform. In Lombardy-Venetia, bureaucratic and financial problems in all levels of government – from the central government in Vienna to the villages of the Venetian provinces – thwarted the process of decision-making and the execution of government orders. Even debates over reform became interminable, and effective action was frustrated by the lack of adequate information.[14]

It is perhaps in this way that the absence of more institutionalised channels of representation (through elections and parliaments), or of a free press, posed the greatest problems. The process of 'consulting' society in Restoration Italy was slow, inefficient and frequently unrepresentative; governments failed to respond to new economic interests also because they simply did not know what these interests were. The systems of congregations often ended in domination by the old nobility, and these too seem to have produced excessive bureaucratisation rather than a responsive and modern central administration. The Austrian government kept the imperial accounts secret, which allowed nationalists to fuel (and perhaps exaggerate) resentment at high levels of taxation.[15] Hence, the absence of open or effective representative institutions prevented governments from broadening their basis of consent. As their successors in Italy and Europe were later to realise, parliaments, elections and a free press were no barrier at all to the construction of a strong state with a powerful bureaucracy and police force; indeed representation and centralisation could go hand in hand. In this respect, the fundamental mistake of Restoration rulers was to attempt a process of political modernisation without touching the traditional structures of deference, authority and personal rule.

Conservative reformers in the Restoration states were, on the whole, unable to establish a broad consensus for reform. It is worth noting that they did little to organise their generally strong basis of support amongst the peasantry. Popular counter-revolutionary militias, such as the *calderai* in the Two Sicilies and the centurions in the Papal States, were organised, but they tended to be used by reactionaries rather than by conservative reformers. In general, conservative reformers greatly feared popular militias for their association with revolutionary violence. So any form of popular militia was believed to be unreliable and inherently unstable, a threat to social order and a challenge to the legitimacy of the state.[16] Here too, we can observe on the part of Restoration rulers an inability to understand the changes wrought by the French Revolution and the effects of their own reforms, and a failure to appreciate the need for new social policies to keep peasants and the poor on their side.

The tensions created by administrative modernisation also gave rise to conflict within the governments themselves. Studies of Lombardy and Venetia confirm the extent to which conflicts of interest inside government administrations undermined the process of reform. Undoubtedly the most crucial factor frustrating reform was the hostility between conservative reformers and reactionaries. For a brief period after the Naples revolution of 1820, the notoriously reactionary Prince of Canosa was made minister of police and led a 'White Terror' against the liberals of his own class and administration. Cardinal Consalvi's efforts between 1814 and 1823 to create a more up-to-date administration for the Papal States were attacked by the reactionary zealots led by Severoli and Pacca from within his own government. When the zealots gained the upper hand with the election of Leo XII to the Papacy, Consalvi was immediately dismissed and his reforms revoked. Prospero Balbo's more timid attempts at legislative reform in Piedmont during 1819–20 were also rejected and defeated by an alliance of reactionaries led by the King.[17]

The idea of administrative monarchy was always controversial and never gained widespread acceptance. For example, despite pressure from the European Powers, Pope Gregory XVI simply rejected all calls for reform in the Papal States. He refused to open access to the higher posts of the papal bureaucracy or to consider any reduction in ecclesiastical privileges. Still, while reactionaries resisted change, demands for reform went unsatisfied and pressure for more radical change built up. As a result, conservative reformers in Italy found themselves fighting a dangerous battle on two fronts: against reactionaries for whom their policies were far too radical and against revolutionaries for whom their policies were far too timid.

In the end, the economic and social crisis of the mid-1840s overwhelmed the process of conservative reform, and contributed significantly to the outbreak of revolution in the spring of 1848. After the 1848–49 revolutions, everything changed. Conservative reformers were marginalised, and all the Restoration governments apart from Piedmont adopted more reactionary policies. Strict censorship was imposed and more elaborate spy networks were established; some revolutionaries from 1848 were summarily tried and executed, and many were sent to prison or forced into exile. Repression, in this period, destroyed all attempts at amalgamation and compromise. Government efforts to establish systems of economic or commercial co-operation were abandoned. It is now generally agreed that Restoration Italy lost its way after 1849, as government took on a more despotic character and rulers suffered a severe crisis of legitimacy. This crisis, along with the faltering of their ally and protector, Austria, was to climax and conclude with disastrous results in 1859–60.

Defeat or victory?

Conservative reformers in the Restoration governments tended to oscillate between old and new, producing a fragile and often inconsistent process of reform. The kinds of political compromises they sought were inherently difficult to reach or to implement. Internal conflicts within administrations, the lack of adequate representative structures, unwieldy bureaucracies and tensions between centre and periphery all undermined conservative reform in Restoration Italy.

None of these structural problems, however, can fully explain why conservative reform became untenable and the Restoration states collapsed in 1859–60. Two additional factors, both relating specifically to the final years of the Restoration (1849–59), need to be considered. First, as mentioned above, the social and economic crisis of the 1840s, culminating in the 1848 revolutions, afterwards gave the upper hand in the Restoration states to reactionaries, entirely halting the process of reform and creating an even graver political and social crisis. Second, the changing international climate of the 1850s, and specifically the decline of Austrian power, favoured liberal-national movements and further undermined the legitimacy of Restoration governments. It is worth remembering that Restoration Italy did not simply sink under the weight of its internal contradictions but was actually defeated, diplomatically and militarily, in 1859–60 by an international coalition directly primarily against Austria. Thus, the long-term failure (or inability) of Restoration governments to pursue independent and successful foreign policies played an equally crucial role in their downfall.

Despite all these problems, it is worth noting that Piedmont, one of the governments which had introduced effective reforms before 1848 and which perhaps came closest to the ideal of an administrative monarchy, did survive the traumas of 1848–49 and proved more than able to manipulate the international situation to its own advantage. It is in the context of finding a middle way between reform and reaction, of establishing a stable and broadly acceptable process of political and administrative modernisation, that the experience of Piedmont after 1849 is so significant.

Piedmont had the advantage, not shared by other Restoration states, of relative independence from Austria and France. This independence gave the government an opportunity (gravely over-estimated by Carlo Alberto in 1848–49 but cleverly used by Cavour in the 1850s) to attract nationalist support for the regime through an anti-Austrian foreign policy. In domestic policy too, the Piedmontese government managed to achieve a more permanent degree of institutional stability and bureaucratic modernisation, as well as relative social stability (guaranteed by an efficient police force). Since Carlo Alberto's government included many conservative reformers and comparatively few reactionaries, a stable consensus in favour of reform was also gradually established. Consequently, the programme of reform pursued under Carlo Alberto could be implemented quite rapidly and was able to attract a limited amount of support from the middle class and the liberal nobility. As a result – and this is perhaps the most crucial difference between Piedmont and the other Restoration states – the liberal dedication to reform in Piedmont also came to involve a commitment to the Savoy monarchy.

During the 1850s, the Piedmontese prime minister Cavour was able to expand this programme to achieve a new and highly dynamic 'amalgam' of absolutism and liberalism, one that represented a viable alternative both to Restoration government and to republican nationalism. Like conservative reformers, moderate liberals feared revolutionary violence and believed in establishing a middle way between revolution and reaction. Unlike them, however, moderate liberals recognised that a constitution that placed legal limits to absolute power, and a parliament that secured effective representation and built new forms of consent, were essential to establishing an effective and sustainable process of political change.

It was precisely this constitutional alternative, embodied by Piedmont, which was able to bring about the downfall of Restoration government elsewhere in Italy and to restructure the rest of the peninsula in its political image. The victory of Piedmont shows that it was possible to reform and strengthen Restoration government, and that a compromise between modernity and tradition could be achieved. Above all, Piedmont's success in 1859–60 suggests that Cavour was not wrong to believe that parliament, a free press, economic growth and a successful foreign policy were the key to achieving a political compromise between the old and the new. And its success tells us that national unification was also about state-making and state-breaking, and about war and diplomacy; and that there was by 1859 something of a power vacuum in the Italian peninsula which the Piedmontese liberals stepped into.[18]

Conservative reformers in the other Restoration states had also taken on the task of building a modern centralised state with an efficient, loyal bureaucracy and some form of territorial control, but they had not succeeded. Ultimately, they failed because they could not win over the reactionaries, nor did they extend representation sufficiently to those new segments of society whose support was vital. They were also not in a position to establish an independent foreign policy. Under attack from revolutionaries and liberals, and despised by reactionaries, faced with economic and territorial difficulties and a growing financial crisis, these conservative reformers proved unequal to the task that faced them. But their defeat was also the failure of their rulers. By the 1850s, with the reform programmes in tatters, the Restoration governments of Italy

Figure 3.2   Camillo Benso Count of Cavour.
William Brockeden, pencil and chalk, 1835. © National Portrait Gallery, London, UK.

Cavour, prime minister of Piedmont and the prime minister of Italy, was a
very different kind of political leader from Mazzini or Garibaldi: cynical,
sophisticated and from a noble background. This drawing of Cavour as a
young man was made during his travels around Europe during the 1830s.

had become isolated internationally, unpopular internally and were still unable to co-operate with each other.

But the failure of conservative reform in Italy meant that the challenge facing Risorgimento liberals was not simply one of ousting the reactionary enemies of liberty and nationhood. Having done this, they also needed to resolve the political contradictions that had overwhelmed the Restoration states. In this sense, the solution of a united Italy was hardly a solution at all. All that Italian liberals achieved before 1860 was the establishment of a broad but basic consensus among some elites in favour of reform. They had still to make firm and stable administrative links between the new state and society, find a cohesive basis of social support and assert Italy's independence abroad. They had to overcome the municipal and regional loyalties that had undermined the reform-ing initiatives of much smaller states before 1860, and they had to build a new set of national institutions as well as a clear sense of national identity. Finally, they had somehow to mend the immensely damaging rift with the Church which was the direct result of national unification. In this way, the internal political struggles that lay at the heart of the Risorgimento were also, and were perhaps most fundamentally, a struggle against the realities of Italy itself.

4

Social Conflict and Social Change

A bourgeois revolution?

There is a long tradition that identifies the Risorgimento with the aspirations and the material interests of the Italian middle classes. This tradition reflects broader historical interpretations that identify the nineteenth century with 'bourgeois progress', and it also reflects political controversies between left and right within Italian history. A non-political approach to the Risorgimento, which explains national unification in terms of social and economic developments, has much to recommend it. It provides a point of departure from an older nationalist school of Risorgimento historiography, which considered only the political, military and diplomatic efforts of a heroic elite; it allows us to broaden our investigation to include the slower, structural developments occurring alongside these more spectacular events; and it pays attention to those who were not leaders, or not even followers, and to their experience of historical change. An approach which focuses on society, not politics, offers us a very different view of the Risorgimento.

Yet this identification of the Risorgimento with bourgeois revolution suffers from acute definitional problems. Who were the Italian middle classes? Where were they to be found and how did they develop and identify themselves? How and when did they carry out this 'bourgeois revolution'? How liberal was their revolution, however it is defined? The lack of clear answers to any of these questions has meant that for many historians of the Risorgimento working within this framework, the Italian experience can only be explained as a deviation from liberal middle-class norms, or as a case of failed bourgeois revolution.

The idea of the Risorgimento as a bourgeois revolution can be traced to the political disputes of the late nineteenth century.[1] As part of a debate about the political legacy of the Risorgimento, the anarchist Francesco Saverio Merlino argued that the problems of unification were the result of class conflict, notably conflict between peasantry and bourgeoisie and between bourgeoisie and aristocracy. Later, in the first decades of the twentieth century, a number of historians began to emphasise the role played by economic factors in the Risorgimento. For example, a 1920 study of Cavour and the moderate liberals attributed their political achievements to their economic success, and specifically to their basis in a new agrarian middle class which formed in Piedmont during the years after 1815.[2] At the same time, a class analysis began to be used to account for the divergence between the perceived achievements of northern Italy and the corresponding failure of the South. Southern Italy's persistent poverty, the absence of industrialisation and the problems of political corruption and stagnation – all this began to be explained by reference to the absence of an industrial or commercial bourgeoisie, the continued dominance of the feudal nobility and a lasting tendency to invest any surplus capital in land.

Two studies combined to establish the new terms of debate on the Risorgimento. The first was Kent Greenfield's *Economics and Liberalism in the Risorgimento*, published in 1934. Focusing on Lombardy, Greenfield emphasised the links between economic development and social change, on the one hand, and the spread of liberal-national ideas, on the other.[3] However, Greenfield's research on Lombardy also led him to conclude that the strongest impetus for the Risorgimento in this region came not from the bourgeoisie, but from landowners and intellectuals who were often aristocrats. Thus, although the Risorgimento was shaped by economic change, the middle class was not responsible for it. Indeed, Greenfield found most merchants and business men in Lombardy to be fundamentally conservative and wedded to traditional habits; far from being risk-taking entrepreneurs, they invested in land, the traditional source of power and status, as soon as they acquired any capital. Far from being the driving force behind economic growth and progress, merchants were no more than passive participants in a world that changed around them.

A pervasive sense of the 'peculiarities' of the Italian bourgeoisie became fundamental to social analyses of the Risorgimento, a sense that class conflict ought to have drive the Risorgimento forward, but was unable to, and that social and economic change lay behind the political developments of the period, but was somehow frustrated. This perspective was developed most fruitfully in a second major study of Italian society, written by the Marxist activist Antonio Gramsci. It was Gramsci in the 1920s and '30s who first defined the Risorgimento as a failed bourgeois revolution. He identified a series of weaknesses in the process of unification in Italy, weaknesses that he attributed to the inability of the middle class to lead a successful revolutionary struggle against the old regime. The absence of a revolutionary middle class meant that the Risorgimento lacked a mass following and, in particular, it lacked a following among the peasantry, the largest section of the Italian population. 'The Italian bourgeoisie', Gramsci wrote, 'was incapable of uniting the people around itself, and this was the cause of its defeat and the interruptions in its development.'[4] Therefore, the Risorgimento became a 'passive revolution' or a revolution without mass participation. The middle class in Italy had not been strong enough to overthrow the existing feudal order and had instead sought a compromise with it, a compromise which worked to exclude the mass of the population and divert the process of change.

As a result of the 'passive revolution', bourgeois rule in Italy could not be 'hegemonic' (based on intellectual, cultural or moral leadership) but had instead to rely on 'domination' (on the state's power of coercion and repression). In a similar way, domination came to characterise relations between the various parts of Italy, notably the relationship between the North and the South. So, for Gramsci, the Italian middle class was not a success in any sense. He also emphasised their difference from the middle classes elsewhere in Europe, and he compared the revolution in Italy unfavourably to the French Revolution in order to show how far the Italians had failed to conform to an established ideal of class leadership. The French Jacobins, who were the political leaders of the French middle classes, had pushed the revolution forward, and they had defeated their enemies who sought to halt the forward march of progress: the Jacobins had, as Gramsci puts it, 'created the bourgeois state [and] made the bourgeoisie into the leading, hegemonic class of the nation'. Risorgimento revolutionaries had done none of these things.[5]

This analysis of the shortcomings of class struggle and revolutionary leadership in the Risorgimento relies on a set of assumptions about progress and change. It accepts that the links between social, economic and political change are, or normally should be, straightforward and that, in Italy, their absence can provide us with an explanation of the peninsula's atypical development in the nineteenth century. The importance of class (whether bourgeoisie, aristocracy or peasantry) and class conflict is also taken for granted, whether as a reason for popular unrest, new political movements or the differences between North and South. It also assumes a single, backward southern society, entirely distinct from and subordinate to the North (this issue is dealt with in the next chapter). Equally, the model fits in well with a more general Marxist interpretation of nineteenth-century European history, that identifies the rise of the bourgeoisie in Europe with a 'dual' economic and political revolution and, specifically, with industrialisation and liberalism which are seen as twin processes. Eric Hobsbawm, a leading proponent of this interpretation, writes that

> the bourgeoisie of the third quarter of the nineteenth century was overwhelmingly 'liberal'. . . . They believed in capitalism, in competitive private enterprise, technology, science and reason. They believed in progress, in a certain amount of representative government, [and] a certain amount of civil rights and liberties.[6]

Hence, the failure of the bourgeoisie to rise to power in Italy can be placed in the wider context of the failure in Italy of liberalism and, in this way, class becomes both analysis and justification. Class describes the social structure of nineteenth-century Italy, the relations between rich and poor and between property-owners and the dispossessed, and it also describes how these relationships changed;

but class also explains Italy's problems: political illiberalism, economic failure and a great deal more besides.

This identification of the bourgeoisie with capitalism, industrialisation and liberalism, and with them the dual revolution in Europe, has been steadily eroded in recent years. One influential trend has been the disintegration of the European norm with which Italy was compared so unfavourably. For instance, the political subordination of the middle class to the aristocracy seems to have been characteristic of most European states until at least the final years of the nineteenth century, and this makes the Italian case more typical than exceptional.[7] Seen in this light, the anomalous features of the Italian middle classes, such as its tendency to invest in land or to blend with the old aristocracy, no longer seem like anomalies at all. Even the political attitudes and political development of the middle classes in Italy now seem, if anything, to reflect broader trends. More recent research has shown that a dual economic and political revolution did not really take place anywhere, and that the most economically successful middle classes, for example in parts of Germany, were rarely the most liberal. The broader European experience shows instead that there were few causal connections between the emergence of bourgeois civil society, the development of industrial capitalism and the establishment of a liberal parliamentary regime, and that these processes could often take place quite independently of each other, in different times and places.[8]

A huge amount of research on the European bourgeoisie has revealed the great diversity of bourgeois activities and bourgeois types. The term 'bourgeois' no longer refers merely to economic activity or, in particular, to an involvement with industry. Instead, the term is often used as a definition of status or to describe a set of ideas or cultural standards. In this broader definition of the middle class, far more attention is paid to the rural middle classes, and to the role played by the professions, or more generally by the non-business world, in promoting middle-class values or interests. An interest in the so-called *petite bourgeoisie*, in shopkeepers, clerks and artisans demonstrates the existence of internal hierarchies and different activities within the ranks of the middle classes, and the variety of ways of becoming and being middle class. In Italy, the bourgeoisie are now more often referred to as the 'middle orders' (*ceti medi*), a category that refers to status rather than to economic function.[9] Equally, it is common to talk of 'notables' or 'elites'; again these are non-economic categories that draw no rigid distinction between the aristocracy and the middle orders.

The proliferation of studies on the Italian middle classes has reflected, and contributes to, this broader reassessment in European history. While earlier work focused on the failings of the Italian bourgeoisie and the disappointment of national unification, a new approach has emerged that emphasises the breadth and diversity of the Italian 'middle orders' and looks beyond those groups who were involved in liberal or nationalist politics. So rather than being judged in terms of their success or failure as a ruling class, the activities of the Italian middle classes are now viewed as part of a much broader process of change and modernisation; and they are studied for their own sake rather than for what they can explain about nationalist politics. Historians have also stressed the continuities between the activities, attitudes and behaviour of the Risorgimento middle classes (1815–70) and those of post-unification and liberal Italy (1870–1914).

In this new context, the link between the Italian middle classes and Italian unification begins to look very tenuous. That is, by dissolving the connections between society and politics, this approach has loosened the causal link between middle class and Risorgimento, and the corresponding centrality of the Risorgimento for middle-class Italy has also been downgraded. As a result, it seems impossible to explain the Risorgimento by using a class-based analysis.

Class, status and power

An important source of power and status throughout Restoration Italy and, later, in Liberal Italy too, was the state. In the absence of industrialisation or other forms of rapid economic change, the attempt to establish modern administrative and juridical systems was probably the most important cause of societal transformation in this period.

Employment in the bureaucracy was a source of social advancement, particularly for university graduates, and in many parts of early nineteenth-century Italy a 'humanist' (educated, professional) bourgeoisie did emerge. However, its identity and activity was strictly circumscribed.[10] Since most of the Restoration states restricted access into the highest ranks of the bureaucracy, reserving the most prestigious and powerful jobs for the sons of the nobility, the most significant employment prospects and avenues of advancement were provided not by the central government but by local administrations.

Perhaps above all in the Southern Italian provinces and in Sicily, employment in local administration and involvement in local politics provided an important measure of status and social mobility. Indeed, for the large number of graduates produced by Southern universities, and often for merchants and landowners as well, a position in the local administration became the easiest means of acquiring wealth, status and security. The powers allocated to local administration – the control over taxation, public works, bureaucratic appointments and, crucially, over the partition of common land – offered to those in charge significant opportunities for patronage and for the direct accumulation of private wealth; so, in this period, the provincial bourgeoisie in many parts of Southern Italy was able to establish robust sources of power through the exercise of routine administrative tasks, and, by controlling access to these tasks, build an equally impressive web of patronage and clientele networks.[11] Nor was this purely a Southern phenomenon. For example, the behaviour of agrarian elites in the Po Valley during and after unification indicates the extent to which, in the North as well, involvement in local politics became a vital means of establishing networks of power and influence.[12]

This picture of local advancement suggests that it was political rather than economic change which produced social mobility in many parts of Italy. At the least it tells us that there was no single factor shaping the new social structures, but instead a whole series of distinct processes which affected each other differently, depending on the local or regional context. Politics and the professions, as well as agriculture, trade and industry, were all overlapping bases for the formation of new elites, and their relative success or failure was often determined by local conditions. What was missing was any national standard or norm.

Perhaps the most obvious manifestation of these social changes was the transformation of land ownership. The rapid economic decline of the Venetian nobility during the eighteenth century and afterwards led to the transfer of land on a large scale to merchants, bankers and *rentiers*. In Sicily, a similar crisis amongst the old aristocracy meant that an increasing amount of land was owned by its former rent collectors. The sale of Church and common land also increased the amount of land available for purchase. Thus, in commercial centres such as Milan and Turin, and in port cities like Livorno and Catania, wealthy merchants bought up this land as a means of acquiring security and status. For similar reasons, rich bureaucrats and lawyers from the major administrative towns also tended to invest widely in property. Land ownership expanded and became a middle-class phenomenon.

Although those who bought land in Venetia and Sicily tended to adopt the traditional practices and social habits of their departed predecessors, this was never invariably the case. For instance, the major social distinction that emerged in the Venetian countryside in the early nineteenth century was based not on class but on the difference in work practices: between those who sought to introduce more efficient and more commercial methods into agriculture and those who did not.[13] Elsewhere, especially in the silk-growing regions and in Tuscany and Umbria, the new landowners tended to be both culturally and socially innovative and economically enterprising. At the same time, members of the old nobility could also be at the forefront of experimentation and innovation. Before becoming involved in liberal politics during the 1840s, both Bettino Ricasoli in Tuscany and Camillo Cavour in Piedmont pioneered attempts to improve production methods on their ancestral estates. Ricasoli also set up road-building schemes and schemes to house and educate the peasants on his land. Yet we must be careful not to extrapolate from a few famous examples. On the whole, the Tuscan nobility tended to be politically progressive but quite averse to financial innovation and to the introduction of capitalist methods in agriculture; instead, they often adopted a conservative economic programme intended to preserve and consolidate the traditional relations of power in the countryside.[14]

During the nineteenth century, numerous setbacks notwith-standing, the new elites steadily accumulated wealth. Various strat-egies were adopted in order to build up capital, status and power but probably the most important mechanism – or at least the one that has been most researched by historians – was the family. If land ownership continued in this period to be the most significant measure of wealth, then family ties and inheritance were the means by which this wealth was secured and increased. The reliance on land ownership and the use of kinship structures has often been taken by some historians to be evidence of the feudal practices and atavistic attitudes of the Italian middle classes. However, more recent work suggests that such apparently tradi-tional practices were often used as a means of promoting specifi-cally capitalist and modernising interests.

Similar strategies provided a means of 'fusing' with old aristo-cratic families, a process which can be taken as proof of the more dynamic and enterprising qualities of the Italian middle classes. It was, above all, in the major cities – where the greatest opportuni-ties for social ties with traditional power-holders existed – that the process of fusion between aristocracy and middle classes to form a broad ruling elite took place most rapidly. Educational, cultural and philanthropic societies, agricultural and scientific organisations, as well as more explicitly economic bodies such as chambers of commerce, were established and attracted an increasingly diverse membership from men of different social origin. During the 1830s, a cosmopolitan group of young aristocrats in Turin (led by Cavour, the Count Ruggiero di Salmour, Carlo Alberto Alfieri and Costantino Nigra) began to seek more open associational networks between the bourgeoisie and the aristocracy. This new associational culture was often explicitly modelled on the examples set by Paris and London.[15] Milan, in particular, developed as a major cultural and intellectual centre at this time, and its social liveliness led many contemporaries to compare the city to Paris.

In the absence of effective political representation, a parallel public space based on clubs, journals and reading often developed. Above all in the principal cities of the North, a profound change occurred to the ways in which social space was used and enjoyed.[16]

This bourgeois, secular public sphere, which developed rapidly during the 1830s and 1840s, revolved around clubs, cafés, theatres and the press, rather than around family, community and the church. It provided opportunities for members of the various elites to meet and mingle in a new environment.

There are still some aspects of the development of bourgeois culture in Italy which remain unstudied. Very little is known about the process of secularisation or about levels of religiosity among the middle classes. It is clear that in common with most of bourgeois Europe, the new public sphere defined itself partly by whom it excluded, and those who did participate in this wider public space still tended to come from the most privileged sections of the middle classes. On the whole, only wealthy merchants and the most successful professionals joined clubs, participated in scientific societies or socialised with the aristocracy. Members of the *petite bourgeoisie* were excluded from these networks, as were women, confined largely to the private sphere of family and home. In this latter case, middle-class sociability represented a restriction on female activity, and a backward step from the salons of eighteenth-century life. Regional variations, finally, were very significant. Thus, there were few clubs, cultural associations and academies in Naples, although theatre played a central role in elite sociability both in the capital and the provinces and private salons continued to thrive well into the middle of the nineteenth century.[17]

Levels of mobility and sociability in the public sphere should also not be overestimated, and in assessing the impact of social mobility on people's lives, we should pay equal attention to developments in the private sphere. Aristocratic resistance to middle-class advancement could drastically curtail, or at least control and redirect, the process of fusion. The experience of smaller towns such as Parma, Lucca and Pisa (in the Grand Duchy of Tuscany) show that in the absence of a new middle class, the old elites were able to maintain their monopoly of power and status well into the 1840s and 1850s. Elsewhere in Tuscany, and perhaps especially at the higher levels of power, the nobility used a variety of new and old strategies – their economic power, their control of moderate politics and the new associational life – to construct a hegemonic system of clientele and friendship networks which enabled them to maintain their supremacy in a changing social and political world.[18] In some cases, where the aristocracy had entered a period of long-term economic decline, as in major cities such as Rome and Palermo which experienced little economic or demographic growth, the middle class was also too insignificant to be able to make contacts with the aristocracy. Here, moreover, the aristocracy jealously guarded its remaining privileges and power. One hostile observer wrote in 1838 of the 'feudal, corrupt and arrogant' atmosphere in Palermo, while thirty years later another commentator referred disparagingly to the nobility's 'unhealthy obsession' with owning fine carriages.[19]

In many regions, traditional rivalries still prevailed and divided members of the old nobility. At least in some cities (Naples, Turin), a new form of stratification emerged where the most powerful noble families kept themselves socially and culturally apart from both the lesser nobility and the rich middle class. Despite the best efforts of Cavour and his friends, the gentlemen's clubs in Turin remained divided along class lines, with the old aristocracy and the rich bourgeoisie co-existing in separate clubs side by side, rather than really intermingling. The Neapolitan noble families maintained their cultural and ideological distance from the middle class, even as aristocratic men entered the bourgeois, public world of business and finance. Above all in the private sphere of family and home, the distinction between modern and traditional behaviour, between what was bourgeois and what was noble, could be rigidly maintained. The home became a symbol of lost order, a personal haven, in a rapidly changing and sometimes violent public world.[20]

Even so, the division between public and private could be hard to sustain: in some cases, politics invaded family life, disrupting traditional relations, creating new tensions and altering accepted gender roles. In particular, when members of the nobility and/or the new elites were active in democratic politics, and especially when they faced hardship or exile as a result of these beliefs, the lives of their families – and the women in them – were deeply affected. Women might take on new roles in the family and outside of it, and could become involved, and active in, the creation of new social and political spaces.[21]

Numerous forms of stratification, the degree of variation between regions and between localities, and the differences between families and between individuals present a complicated picture to historians. It is also difficult to reach firm conclusions about the political implications of these changes. The emergence of new public spaces is generally associated with the development of liberal public opinion in Europe, and there is much evidence for this in some Italian cities; first in Milan and Florence in the early Restoration period, then most rapidly and visibly in liberal Turin during the 1850s. In other cases, however, very little changed. Elsewhere again, research provides as much evidence of a growth of tension, disagreement and fracture – in other words, of a renewal of conflict for control of the new public spaces and opportunities in spite of the additional scope they offered.

The new administrative institutions of the early Restoration period often became the target of considerable middle-class resentment, either because they were inefficient or autocratic or because employment in the higher ranks was dominated by the old nobility. In a few famous cases this discontent translated into active liberal opposition against the existing regimes. As we saw in the previous chapter, the restriction of opportunities for bureaucratic employment by the Austrians in Lombardy-Venetia, and the attempt in Piedmont to purge the army of its liberal elements, gave an important boost to liberal opposition movements in northern Italy. Here a relatively clear-cut dispute between state and civil society emerged. In other respects, however, the adjustments of the Restoration period produced more subtle, and more complex, kinds of social and political tensions. These tensions could undermine political stability by producing rivalries within communities as different groups fought for access to the bureaucracy or the possibilities of power and money that it offered. Conflicts between families, factions and friends, as well as between social classes, were often the result.

One effect of the Bourbon administrative reforms in southern Italy was to produce solidarity within communities, with elites coming together to resist the effect of these changes imposed by the central government from outside. Rapidly, however, this cohesion was eroded as new landed and commercial elites came to compete with the old ruling class for the resources and privileges also assigned by the central government.[22] In many parts of the South, these kinds of conflicts then exploded into communal violence. Particularly during moments of political turmoil – for example during the revolutions of 1820, 1848 and 1860 – members of the new elites attempted to seize control of the local administration by force. The National Guards, established during the liberal revolutions of 1848 and 1860 to protect private property and promote middle-class power, were even used as private armies at this time to support or impose rival political claims.

Personal rivalries had direct consequences for the public sphere. In Sicily, both sides used criminal gangs and bandits in order to reinforce their political claims and to protect or increase their property and wealth. Bandits were 'employed' by powerful families to exact revenge on their enemies, to steal cattle and generally to accumulate power; banditry was linked to powerful political and class interests and became an entrenched part of rural life in Sicily, so that behind every bandit, it was claimed, 'there was always the figure of a nobleman, a judge, a mayor or a police chief'.[23] This situation produced political instability, social tensions, violence and factionalism rather than liberal opposition movements. And in this context, liberal and/or nationalist movements had little relevance and could provide still less a basis for collective action.

So it is very hard to generalise about the overall effects of social mobility in Italy in the first half of the nineteenth century. The emergence of new elites did involve the creation of new economic opportunities and different forms of social interaction. However, this development was not always accompanied by respect for the rule of law, a sense of national identity or a commitment to the principles of liberal political economy. If, at one extreme, the middle orders and aristocracy of Milan mingled and socialised in theatres, clubs and cafés, at the other extreme, in the isolated towns and villages of Western Sicily, competing elites battled against each other, using all the economic, political, personal and social weapons at their disposal. It is far from clear why structural change produced elite violence in Sicily and forms of sociability in Milan, although it seems likely that this kind of elite behaviour in rural Sicily was a response to restricted economic opportunities and the correspondingly fierce competition for political resources made available by the state.[24] What is evident is that, in most parts of Italy, liberalism and nationalism did not go hand in hand with the growth of a middle-class society.

The rise of rural unrest

If the identification of the Risorgimento with the interests and aspirations of the middle class is not sustainable, then we also need to reconsider the role played by class conflict. The thrust of much recent research has been to downplay the importance of class conflict in the Risorgimento and, in particular, to deny any connection between popular revolt and political attitudes. Moreover, historical studies of crime and popular disorder elsewhere in Europe suggest, once again, that there was nothing at all exceptional about Italy. That is, social problems resulting from rapid urbanisation and escalating rural poverty, along with an apparent rise in crime and the spread of epidemic disease, were common to most European states in this period. They were certainly not an exclusively Italian problem.

In his classic study of the Risorgimento, Gramsci argued that the threat of popular revolution so alarmed the Italian bourgeoisie that it led them to seek compromises with the existing feudal order. In turn, he argued, the lack of a popular alliance with the mass of the population fatally undermined the revolution of the Italian middle classes and can explain the chronic social unrest in the Risorgimento period. But does this analysis account for the complex character of social change and the varieties of popular unrest in the Risorgimento? Does the specific nature of its class conflict and class alliances set Italy apart from other European societies, and explain the problems of the Risorgimento and its aftermath? Before we can answer these questions, it is necessary to look at the sources of tensions and problems amongst the rural and urban poor.

The growth of the so-called 'dangerous classes' in both rural and urban Italy was part of a much broader European trend. The legal and economic reforms of the late eighteenth century, greatly accelerated during the revolutionary and Napoleonic periods, had dramatic social consequences which were initially felt most strongly in the countryside. The dismantling of feudal structures led to changes in land ownership and to the growth of new agrarian classes. An important consequence of these changes was the rapid erosion of customary land-use rights enjoyed by the peasantry. In Italy, this process took place very rapidly and can be connected to the equally rapid spread of peasant disturbances.

Although these land-use rights differed from one agricultural region to another in Italy, they all provided a means by which peasant families could supplement their income from their own meagre plots of land or from salaried work. One of the most important rights was the right to graze livestock on common land. Others included access to a water supply (particularly important in the arid South), to forestry for the collection of dead wood and, in the coastal wetlands, to the marshes for the gathering of straw and canes. These rights, often together with seasonal migration, sustained impoverished rural communities and protected their inhabitants from destitution.

The enclosure of common land and its conversion into leasehold or freehold property, along with the abolition of rights of forage and grazing, led to drastic changes for the Italian peasantry. One clear effect of the destruction of land-use rights was to give rise to a new differentiation within rural communities. In some regions, peasants were able to acquire a part of the leasehold property for themselves. Perhaps most notably in the Piedmontese hill zones, and in other mountainous areas, a class of independent, small peasant proprietors distinct from the poor landless labourers did emerge. But elsewhere, if peasant farmers were able to buy land, they often lacked the means to make it profitable. Generally uneducated and without any capital to improve their land, these peasants then fell rapidly into debt and were forced to sell to speculators who, in turn, sold to large landed proprietors. So, in the event, often the most striking effect of these changes was the creation of ever-larger landed estates owned by single proprietors, along with a class of near-destitute landless labourers.

In the Lombard and Venetian plains, the impact of the loss of land rights led to a dramatic deterioration in the peasantry's economic position. In the areas of intense commercial activity in Lombardy, a class of proletarianised wage-labourers (*braccianti*) replaced sharecropping farmers.[25] The decision of the Vienna government in 1839 to declare all uncultivated common land available for private purchase dealt a devastating blow to many rural communities, and particularly affected by this decree were the rural poor whose livelihood depended on hunting, fishing and gathering cane from the extensive and uncultivated marshlands on the Venetian coast. Advances in land reclamation and drainage techniques also meant that this long-deserted area became attractive to potential investors, and it was rapidly enclosed, drained and placed under cultivation.[26] A similar process took place in the province of Lazio around Rome. Here land enclosures disrupted the pattern of transhumance which had existed for centuries and accentuated the conflict between arable farmers and cattle drovers (*boattieri*). The livelihood of cattle drovers, often a powerful group within such rural communities, was seriously threatened by these changes.[27]

Comparable tensions can be found throughout the South and in the islands. The destruction of the collective rights on which rural communities had long been dependent caused conflict and unrest, and the main target was the landowners who had benefited from the changes.[28] Aside from the terrible hardship caused by the loss of these rights, the central government's promise to compensate peasants by allocating them a portion of enclosed common land created new and equally grave tensions and resentment. In many communities, unscrupulous landowners took advantage of the uncertainty caused by ambiguity in the legislation in order to 'usurp' (claim and illegally enclose) common land for their own private use. These actions, in turn, increased peasant poverty and added to further conflict for control and ownership of the land.[29]

On the whole, therefore, although there was an increase in the land under cultivation during this period, the effects of land reform were generally disruptive and rarely beneficial to the peasantry. Moreover, the loss of land-use rights was made all the more harmful by the impact of other developments. First, Italy as a whole experienced rapid, if sporadic, population growth in this period which increased pressure on the land. Second, the growing scale of peasant indebtedness paralysed the peasant economy. Since many small peasant landholders and sharecroppers were unable to support themselves by themselves, they relied more and more on loans of various kinds to last from harvest to harvest. It appears that many of the newly enriched landowners and their agents demanded far more usurious rates of interest from their peasant debtors than their aristocratic predecessors ever had. As a result, and throughout Italy, peasants became trapped in an endless cycle of poverty and debt repayment from which there was little escape. Government intervention through indirect taxation (salt taxes, grist taxes), stamp duties and military conscription also increased the economic burden on the peasantry.

The vulnerability of rural communities to economic pressure is also acutely demonstrated by the high incidence of famine as well as by the spread of epidemic and endemic diseases in this period. Between 1814 and 1818, in the mid-1840s and again in 1853, widespread famine decimated the rural population. Cases of pellagra (a disease caused by vitamin deficiency, and specifically by a diet based exclusively on maize, which resulted in insanity and sometimes cases of suicide in its victims) were widespread throughout northern Italy. The prevalence of malaria in the summer months depopulated some of the most fertile countryside, transforming it into a deadly, impoverished desert. Probably the most feared disease of all, however, was cholera, which swept with devastating force through the cities and rural areas of Italy between 1835 and 1837, in 1849 and again between 1854 and 1855 (the effects of cholera were felt most strongly in the cities and will be discussed in more detail in relation to the urban poor).

However, despite the widespread hardship and bitter discontent, the extent to which we can directly link the deterioration in the peasants' economic position to their participation (or lack of participation) in the Risorgimento is doubtful. Evidence of a wider political awareness can be found, whether in the land agitation organised by Southern peasants in 1848–49, or in the oppositional agitation that developed near Rome in the local bars and *osterie* frequented by 'foreigners' in the same years.[30] In particular, the welcome given by Sicilian peasants to Garibaldi who, in 1860, promised land to all who joined his army, suggests that a political link between the peasants and the liberal-national leadership could have been established, had there been a political will to represent the interests of the rural poor.

However, we should be careful of generalising on the basis of these well-known events. Although the extent of peasant discontent was clearly significant, its existence never guaranteed popular support for revolutionary action in the Risorgimento. Peasant resistance to most forms of political change was as clear in 1848–49 as it was with the Jacobins some fifty years earlier, and even if this opposition could have been overcome, the problem of creating a nationwide movement on the basis of resentments which were overwhelmingly local would have proved almost insuperable.

Within many rural communities, and the breakdown of traditional hierarchies notwithstanding, the persistence of powerful vertical ties – between peasant and noble/peasant and landowner – prevented the emergence of class conflict and class consciousness. The dominant role of the Church in local communities, often embodied by the moral, charitable and educational power of the parish priest, bolstered loyalty to the traditional head of state and undermined political groups that appealed to the secular 'nation'. In this respect, Garibaldi's success with the Sicilian peasantry in 1860 may have been due as much to his careful cultivation of good relations with the Church as to any political sympathy with peasant revolt (which some members of his administration sought actively to repress).[31] Equally, peasant unrest in the South cannot be separated from other economic conflicts in this period: those between arable farmers and cattle drovers over land usage, or the factional struggles for control of local administrations; and in practice class conflict was also intertwined with personal loyalties, local schisms, community tensions or even generational conflict. All these factors suggest that we need to consider peasant unrest as a phenomenon entirely separate from the growth of liberal and nationalist movements during the same period.

Yet although the gulf between nationalist revolution and peasant hardship seems undeniable, we should not conclude that the countryside was remote from, or oblivious to, the broader process of political change. At the local level and across Italy, there was a great deal of peasant resistance to the encroachment on common land,

and an increasing use of direct action (land occupations, public demonstrations) as a form of protest. The use of direct action is especially interesting as it indicates something of a breakdown in old, feudal ties of patronage and deference, and peasant frustration at their lack of an effective voice at the communal level.

The petitions drawn up by the Venetian peasantry in protest at the erosion of land-use right suggest a sense of 'moral economy': they appeal to higher authorities, to a sense of community justice and to traditional rights.[32] In the Roman countryside, the appeal to community justice was also common. Attempts were also made to seek redress through the law: when the enclosure movement was accelerated after 1849, cattle drovers conducted searches in local archives to give a legal basis to their claims.[33] In Sicily, peasant discontent over the land situation was initially encouraged by the new elites, in an effort to bring popular pressure to bear in their own factional struggles. And the involvement of peasants in these conflicts exposed them, in turn, to the language of the law and of radicalism, and often led them to discover a history of their own and become aware of their rights over the land. By the 1840s and thereafter, many peasants began to use this knowledge to vent their growing sense of injustice over the appropriation of common land, to protest at economic conditions and to agitate against their political masters.[34]

National events could alter rural society and the political perceptions of even its poorest inhabitants. For example, the revolutionary changes in one capital city, Rome, during 1848–49 affected rural life across its provinces.[35] The Roman Republic was unique among revolutionary governments of this period in its interest in peasant reform and in rural areas, and it also made new demands on the provinces in terms of active participation and military service. The impact of these changes was quite complex. In some instances, these new impositions were resented by the peasants, while the organisation of national guards and new administrations accentuated community conflict, often to the detriment of the Republic. But in other respects, the political changes in Rome brought about a transformation in the political attitudes and mentalities of local communities. The events leading up to declaration of the Republic in 1849 entailed the establishment of new information networks and signified, for rural communities, the right to form new clubs (*circoli*) and associations and to adopt new forms of public behaviour – to sing patriotic songs, organise patriotic festivals and so on. Political agitation spread rapidly through these new public spaces, where radical discussion and new social networks thrived.[36]

Although this picture of peasant sociability and politicisation can be challenged,[37] it seems clear that the 1848–49 revolutions in Italy were a watershed moment in the politicisation of the countryside. For the rural poor in the Roman countryside, the arrival of the Republic represented a dramatic collapse of legitimate authority and traditional values. Not everyone welcomed these changes, but they certainly created a definitive break with religious tradition and the older political hierarchy as well as a permanent rift within rural communities – between those who embraced the new, and those who rejected it. The wider implication is that even a failed revolution such as 1848–49 helped to establish the conditions for a crisis of traditional authority and led, in the longer term, to increased political instability. So, political change affected peasant life, but only in local terms and in largely unintended ways.

Attempts to follow Eric Hobsbawm's celebrated, but now widely criticised, interpretation of banditry, and to link it with social protest and political action, have not been particularly successful in the Italian context.[38] Banditry in Italy, like peasant unrest over land, was tied to local conditions rather than to national trends, and most studies fail to find much evidence for politically motivated or class-conscious activity on the part of bandits themselves.[39] In Sicily, bandits existed mainly to serve powerful landlords and nobles, whereas in much of the Southern mainland bandits were involved in independent activities, such as smuggling and cattle rustling, for their own private gain. Arguably, brigandage in Southern Italy had no political ideology at all, and only acquired a political direction as part of the much broader struggle between local communities and the centralising state.[40]

The urban poor

One problem with class-based analyses of the poor is that they tend to assume that protest was the only possible outlet for peasant grievances in this period. In fact, an alternative response was to migrate to the towns. Peasant migration was probably the major reason for the rapid growth experienced by cities such as Milan, Turin and Naples, and the creation there of urban 'dangerous classes'. In these cities, casual work sustained (or failed to sustain) a large section of the poorer classes. Throughout the first half of the nineteenth century, Turin attracted not industrial workers but seasonal bricklayers, artisans, porters, street peddlers, domestic servants and a mass of poor peasants who eked out a marginal existence often dependent on charity and begging.[41] The population of Milan, more of an industrial centre than Turin, also contained a significant portion of casual workers as well as a very high number of shopkeepers and artisans. Even workers in the industrialising textile sector (the bulk of whom were female) were, until the 1850s, usually paid on a part-time basis and did their work from home.

In many respects, the growth of cities such as Milan, Turin and Naples merely continued at an accelerated rate a process that had begun in every major Italian city during the eighteenth century. In the course of the eighteenth century, the population of Turin more than doubled, while in the thirty or so years between the Restoration and the 1848 revolutions Milan's population grew from 139,000 inhabitants to 189,000.[42] In common with many other rapidly expanding cities in Europe at this time, these urban centres lacked either the infrastructure or the employment prospects to support their growing populations. The creation of a 'dangerous class' of casual labourers who lived, according to one contemporary observer, 'in idleness and vagabondage' and constituted 'a permanent danger to social order' has to be understood in this context.[43] The problems of this hungry, marginal class were intensified by economic reforms, such as the abolition of price controls on foodstuffs. Their problems were, in turn, made more visible by the absence, at least until the middle of the century, of any rigid social segregation in housing. The *palazzi* of the rich housed many poor families, while the destitute lived on the streets, intensifying fears among the propertied elites of robbery and food riots.

A substantial proportion of this dangerous class was female. During this period, many married women left their lives of unmitigated drudgery in the countryside, and migrated to the cities of northern and central Italy. In these cities, they found few new opportunities for work. Legally subordinated to men, and discriminated against in terms of education and wages, they tended to take on the most marginal of jobs, often combining domestic service with weaving, needlework and childcare.[44] The growth in infanticide and infant abandonment experienced in this period (the number of infants abandoned in Milan increased five-fold between the 1770s and the 1850s, and in Florence the number grew by 70 per cent during roughly the same period)[45] is a telling indication of the increasing economic pressures on women. Frequently, mothers would place their babies in foundling homes and hope to return, either when better off or when the babies had grown, to retrieve them.

However, in Italy as in London, Paris, Portsmouth or Hamburg, by far the most visible 'dangerous' females were prostitutes. Prostitutes were often, but not always, single women from rural areas, seeking to supplement their meagre incomes as servants, laundresses, seamstresses or waitresses. The prostitute's public presence, the presence of a woman alone and independent of accepted moral standards, on city streets in Italy raised a host of fears concerning the effects of urbanisation on the moral, sexual, social and physical health of the population.[46] The association of prostitutes with criminals and vagrants further intensified anxieties about the growth of a criminal underworld beyond the control of rational, civilised society. Prostitutes were also blamed for the spread of venereal disease, particularly amongst the armed forces, and were considered a significant danger to public health.

In fact, besides the perceived spread of crime and disorder in urban areas, disease constituted the major threat to social stability in many towns and cities of Europe. In Italy, urban growth created a speculative boom in property, resulting in the rapid construction of housing that was both unsafe and unsanitary. There were few fire brigades, bad roads and inadequate hospitals. Narrow streets and high buildings, and the absence of green spaces or of a hygienic water supply created ideal conditions for the incubation of disease. Few, if any, towns possessed adequate sanitary facilities. People disposed of their rubbish in the streets which became open sewers, slept in the same damp rooms as their animals and defecated in front of their houses. In the town of Cremona, in

Lombardy, the run-off from the local cemetery was found to have contaminated the water supply.[47]

In such conditions, cholera spread with rapid and tragic results. Two thousand people died of cholera in Genoa during 1835, while those who could fled the city (approximately one-third of the population). In 1837, 13,810 died in Naples and 27,000 people, one-sixth of the total population, died of cholera in Palermo.[48] The spread of cholera is also symptomatic of the wider crisis of urban centres in the nineteenth century. Not knowing the cause of the epidemic, and lacking adequate medical facilities, the authorities were unable to prevent its spread. Italian towns as far apart as Genoa, Livorno, Naples and Palermo experienced riots and demonstrations in the years of cholera epidemics. Riots in Palermo during the 1837 cholera epidemic developed into an anti-Bourbon revolt which spread to the surrounding province and, with the participation of many liberals, eventually to Siracusa and Catania as well. From the 1830s until the 1860s, liberals in the mainland South and Sicily also attempted to use successive cholera epidemics to stir up antigovernment feeling amongst the urban poor, playing on a popular myth which attributed the epidemic to deliberate poisoning. Police controls, imposed by the authorities in an attempt to isolate the disease, merely intensified popular resentment.

Towns and cities were at the centre of all the European revolutions between 1820 and 1871, and Italy was no exception. The problems of Italy's cities in this period – rapid population growth accompanied by the spread of disease and the creation of 'dangerous classes' – were broadly the same as those encountered throughout Europe. It is worth emphasising, therefore, that in Italy as in Europe, all the major urban revolts that took place during this period were not based on these dangerous classes at all, but on the craft workers and artisans.

Artisans were behind the successful popular uprisings in Palermo, Milan, Venice, Livorno and Rome in 1848–49. Unfortunately, we know relatively little about the experiences of artisans and other intermediate groups in the Risorgimento period. Not much is known, for instance, about the participation of artisans in revolutionary organisations such as the National Guards, about their access to Republican networks, or about their participation in volunteer armies in 1848–49, 1859 and 1860.[49] It is, nevertheless, possible to speculate about their motives for revolutionary action. In Italy, although perhaps less than in Europe as a whole, markets for artisanal goods were shrinking due to the influx of cheaper, factory-made, products. As early as 1820, artisans acted in Palermo to protect their corporate privileges which were under attack from government legislation, and to maintain their wage differentials which were being eroded by competition from cheap, rural labour. Increasingly, artisans became dependent on supplying the rich with luxury items, or on satisfying a bourgeois craving for aristocratic style, in order to sustain their livelihoods. They were, therefore, particularly vulnerable to economic downturns. Yet crucially, and in contrast to the more marginal 'dangerous classes', they still possessed in their corporate organisations the means to protest against and to disrupt the new bourgeois society.

Social control and charity

Since the connections between popular revolt and the Risorgimento are both misleading and difficult to establish, many historians have begun to investigate the broader response of Italian elites to the increase in rural poverty and the intensification of urban unrest. These investigations throw new light on how relations between state and society, and between classes, were conducted and understood in this period. A focus on charity reveals how such institutions both reflected and affected the changing problems of urban society. For example, the increase in infant abandonment led, first, to a significant increase in the numbers of foundling hospitals and these, in turn, may have actually encouraged impoverished mothers to abandon their babies.[50] The numbers of poor women seeking assistance in refuges also rose rapidly, perhaps reflecting their increasingly precarious position in society.[51]

Studies of the provision of charity also provide a means of investigating the changing relations between Church, state and society. Much of the charitable assistance available – whether through hospitals, refuges, soup kitchens or loans – was offered by the Church, and was one means by which the Church maintained its power within poor communities. However, in some cities the Church's care of the poor was challenged, first by the initiatives of private citizens and, second, by the state itself. In Turin, the changing focus of charitable work and its removal from religious control was reflected most strongly in the development of an independent educational system, at the instigation of its new urban elite. A number of state-controlled children's schools (*asili infantili*) were established in Piedmont, Tuscany and Naples during the 1840s, with the aim of providing primary instruction for the male children of artisans and the labouring poor. Educational reforms also seem to reflect new bourgeois values. As well as teaching basic literacy skills, an ideal confirmed in the Boncampagni Law (1848) and the Casati Law (1859) in Piedmont, these schools sought to instil values of sobriety, discipline and acceptance of the prevailing social hierarchy.

At the same time, a vigorous public debate on pauperism developed, which reflected the ideological divisions among elites. Opinion was divided between those who argued in favour of private or religious philanthropy and those who argued for state intervention to solve the crisis. These debates also registered a conflict between approaches to poverty, with Malthusian advocates of liberal self-help taking on proponents of Catholic humanitarianism.[52] In other respects, traditional approaches were maintained and, in particular, a distinction continued to be made between the 'deserving poor', those who merited public assistance, and the 'idle poor', the vagrants, beggars and prostitutes from whom society had to be protected. Yet the idle poor also began to be subject to more unequivocal forms of control and treated in a way that is recognisably modern.

In this period, the police acquired new powers of intervention and regulation to deal with the idle poor. In Lombardy, the police were given special powers to prevent the rural poor from entering the towns to beg. The vagrancy law passed in Piedmont in 1829 served a similar purpose. A large number of poorhouses were opened during the 1830s in order to confine those found begging in the towns. Some workhouses, based either on the French or English models, were also established in Piedmont in order to re-educate paupers from their supposed indolence by using them for public work projects, and special legislation was passed to deal with the health risk posed by prostitution. From the 1830s onwards, prostitutes in Naples and Palermo were forced to undergo regular medical inspection. In 1855, a system of licensed brothels was introduced in Piedmont and, under the Piedmontese regulations, those who refused to enter licensed brothels could be arrested while those found to be suffering from a venereal disease were forced to enter syphilitic asylums.[53]

The establishment of paramilitary rural police forces (*carabinieri, gendarmerie*) in most Italian states by the 1830s is also indicative of a preoccupation with pauperism and crime. In some respects, the specific criminalisation of brigandage was symptomatic of a broader process, whereby the judicial authorities sought to control and contain the population of rural areas. Bandits were designated by the political and judicial authorities, and classified as outlaws (*fuor-bandito*) for being a member of an armed gang.[54] In the Two Sicilies, those designated as bandits were condemned to death in their absence, their names were publicly displayed on a list in town squares and highways, and campaigns were mounted to bring them to justice. Bandits thus acquired a unique significance as a symbol of rural lawlessness and as an exceptional threat to civilised society.

The aim of such legislation was to constrain the movement and activity of the 'dangerous' rural and urban poor, and it resulted in increased powers being given to the police. Bandits, vagrants and prostitutes were special categories of criminal, subject to special police controls which, once imposed, were difficult to escape from. In this respect, policies on public order and charity in Restoration Italy reflect an interest in social discipline and an emphasis on surveillance which are typical of modern state formation. And there is plenty of evidence to show that the poor made no distinction between hospitals, refuges, poor houses and prisons: all were seen as places of confinement or death, while the coercive function of public assistance was recognised and resented.

However, perhaps the most interesting conclusion to be drawn from this research is that, despite the powers allocated to both the providers of charity and the police, much charity and police work was ineffective. The distinction between deserving and idle poor was hard to sustain in the changing environments of Restoration Italy. While the police enjoyed extensive powers they lacked, on the whole, sufficient resources to arrest or confine all those perceived to constitute a danger to society. Although the provision of elementary education did lead, in the long term, to a decline in popular illiteracy, huge disparities remained between North and South and between men and women.

It is also clear, finally, that much of this public assistance and police action was misdirected. The insistence on confining the poor to the countryside was not only impracticable but also indicative of a tendency to romanticise rural life and to ignore real social problems. Police action focused on controlling a dangerous class which was, in reality, more helpless than criminal. Respectable artisans, as the 1848 revolutions showed only too visibly, posed a much graver threat to public order. It may also be that heavy-handed policing simply increased elite resentment at government interference while doing nothing to calm their fears of social disorder and crime. The problems of policing and social control, in other words, reflected the broader crisis of Restoration government and the loss of confidence in its capacity to protect the interests of property holders, both new and old.[55]

Social control and Italian unification

The complexities of social change in nineteenth-century Italy make it difficult to establish any clear causal links between changes in the social structure and the process of national unification. In this sense, Gramsci's identification of the Risorgimento with a failed bourgeois revolution cannot be sustained. He relies on a model of national development that fundamentally distorts the locally and regionally based nature of social conflict, and his analysis underestimates the problems of creating a revolutionary movement with a truly national appeal. Moreover, by emphasising class as the motor force of history, Gramsci ignores the crucial role played by politics in the transformation of society. Finally, his notion of 'passive' revolution in Italy relies on a model of successful revolution in France that is highly questionable.

Nevertheless, by pointing to the fear of popular revolution and, more generally, to the prevalent social anxiety of this period,

Gramsci's analysis still offers important insights. The proletarianisation of the rural poor in parts of the North, and the loss of land-use rights by the same in the South indicate a real change in the social structure of the countryside, while the rapid population growth in the cities brought a host of new problems. These changes are reflected in the fear of popular disorder, and they affected the political attitudes of the urban and rural elites. It certainly made them wary of radical change and it clearly bred political discontent. Sporadic riots, robberies and the spectacle of poverty discredited Restoration governments, so apparently unable to enforce public order. Moreover, popular unrest, by adding an extra dimension to existing community conflicts, undermined attempts to modernise government and centralise administrative control.

If it is possible at all to generalise about the political impact of social change, we might conclude that such change left a profound trace at every level of society, in the city and the countryside, but that its impact varied from region to region, from locality to locality and even from family to family. Social mobility produced political instability, but there is a huge gulf between, on the one hand, the capacity of the old Tuscan nobility to adapt to and control their changing world and the factional conflict produced by the arrival of new elites in many parts of the Mezzogiorno. Thus, there was no obvious liberal convergence between the social or economic activities of new elites and the political views adopted by them. Dissatisfaction with government policies did not always translate into active political support for liberal movements. Indeed, demands for local/regional autonomy, fear of popular disorder and a desire for personal aggrandisement often clashed with liberal ideals of national independence, constitutional government and economic progress. It is in this social context that the reversals suffered by liberal-nationalist movements between 1815 and 1860 can be understood. Their successes would seem to require a different explanation.

5

Growth, Stagnation and Economic Difference

Dualism and development

The economic development of Italy between 1815 and 1860 was a central issue in the liberal critique of Restoration government. Italy's old regime rulers were restored in 1815 during a period of acute economic crisis. One effect of the Revolutionary and Napoleonic wars had been severely to damage Italian trade, along with the economies of the major ports, particularly Venice; the aftermath of war saw a Europe-wide economic depression which undermined agricultural production, and many parts of Italy suffered a famine that lasted until 1818. The more positive economic effects of French rule, most notably with regard to infra-structure, also lost momentum with the changes of government in 1815. A sense of economic decline, and of growing economic weak-ness relative to their northern European competitors, dogged Italy's governments up until unification.

This sense of economic backwardness persisted after unification. Partly as a result, a concern with the failure of Italy's economic development in the nineteenth century came to dominate the agenda of Italy's economic historians. They sought explanations, first, for Italy's late and uneven industrial revolution and, second, for the difference between North and South which had become such a persistent feature of the Italian economy since unification. In this way, much of the discussion of Italy's economies in the early nineteenth century was teleological, that is, it sought only to find in the Risorgimento period the origins of late industrialisation or of economic dualism in post-unification Italy. Finally, during the 1950s and 1960s, historical interest in the economies of nineteenth-century Italy also reflected contemporary, post-war concerns with economic growth, the economic disparities between countries and the role of state intervention.[1]

These economic questions had a more general significance in that they formed a central element in the debate between Marxist and liberal historians over the nature of the Risorgimento and the political achievements of liberal Italy. Dominating this debate was a presumed link between weak economic growth and failed political change, and more specifically the link between the failure of economic unification and political unification. At the centre of this debate were three historians, Emilio Sereni, Rosario Romeo and Alexander Gerschenkron, who concerned themselves with the economic implications of Gramsci's analysis.

Sereni, a Marxist, based his account on Gramsci's theory of 'passive revolution', and stressed the weakness of the Italian bourgeoisie and the slow development of industrial capitalism. According to Sereni, Italian industrialisation was retarded by a low level of internal demand, caused by rural poverty and the propensity of the peasant economy toward self-sufficiency. Thus, the slow industrial growth experienced in Italy could be attributed to the failure to modernise Southern agriculture (to 'eradicate [feudal] residues', as Sereni put it) and to increase peasant consumption; without a domestic (peasant) market for Italian manufactured goods, Italian manufacturing could not grow. In short, Sereni argued that Italy's poor economic performance after 1860 could be traced to the defeat of peasant revolution in the South at the time of national unification.[2]

Romeo's starting-point was a rejection of the possibility or desirability of peasant revolution in southern Italy. For Romeo, a right-wing historian, Italy's late industrialisation (in the 1880s) was not caused by low demand but by lack of investment, resulting from problems in the 'original accumulation of capital' (the increase in the amount of capital offered for production purposes). Since this 'original accumulation' required the suppression, not the encouragement, of mass consumption, peasant revolution in the South would have directly hampered the development of industrial capitalism in the North. Moreover, industrialisation in northern Italy was only made possible by the Italian state's direct exertion of fiscal pressure on southern agriculture, and specifically through the extraction of a surplus from agriculture which was then used to build the administrative and commercial infrastructure necessary for industrialisation to take place. Hence, the defeat of peasant revolution in the South and the powerlessness of the rural classes had been crucial to capitalist development, as was the subordination of the southern economy to the interests of the North; so, far from stimulating industrialisation, a successful revolution in the South would have delayed the process still further.[3]

Romeo's account was challenged by the American economist Alexander Gerschenkron. In a chapter of his book, *Economic Backwardness in Historical Perspective,* which dealt with Italy as an industrial 'latecomer', Gerschenkron criticised Romeo's 'original accumulation of capital' thesis. He denied any immediate causal link between the extraction of surplus of agriculture and industrialisation, and argued that it was banks, not the state, which played the crucial role in investment in industry. The results of state intervention in the economy were, Gerschenkron maintained, largely negative; in particular, the protectionist policies pursued after the 1880s probably undermined economic growth in Italy. Arguing from a general model that saw industrialisation developing in a series of abrupt 'stages', with a marked discontinuity between stages, he also located the moment of Italy's industrialisation rather later than Romeo, that is, in the late 1890s. The 1890s were, according to Gerschenkron, the period when Italy experienced what he called its big (if in practice rather weak) 'spurt' of self-sustaining economic growth.[4]

Interest in Italy's economic development during the Risorgimento was long dominated by these disagreements about the industrialisation of liberal Italy in the late nineteenth century. So it is worth noting that they rest on a number of common assumptions. First, these explanations are all mono-causal, that is, they attribute the character of economic development in Italy to a single cause (the failure of bourgeois revolution, the original accumulation of capital, or the action of investment banks).[5] Second, they are based on an economic analysis of a political nation; they assume that countries within political boundaries are the only valid units for considering the process of industrialisation. Third, they take for granted the involvement of national governments in promoting industrialisation and assess it only on the basis of its relative success or failure. In the Italian context, therefore, the persistence of regional economies and regional governments until well into the nineteenth century has logically to be seen as a major disadvantage.

Underlying all the analyses of Italy's economic backwardness and its position as an industrial latecomer is a sense of the 'peculiarities' of the Italian experience. These peculiarities, it is argued, disadvantaged and weakened Italy's economy *vis-à-vis* its apparently more successful European competitors. Thus, analyses of Italy's late, uneven or distorted economic development after 1815 are implicitly comparative, at least in the negative sense. They involve an assessment of the Italian economy in terms of what it lacked when compared to the economies of Britain, France and/or Germany. The absence of heavy industry and the scarcity of modern technology, or the ruralisation of industrial production and the use of a rural labour force – these distinctive features of the Italian economy in the nineteenth century are also seen as key elements in explaining Italy's backwardness.

For example, Italy's late industrialisation was linked to the ruralisation of Italian industries, a process that began in the seventeenth century but was given additional impetus in the nineteenth. Ruralisation was held responsible for the delay in introducing new technology and in the development of factory production. In fact, the ruralisation of industry undermined the competitiveness of Italian manufactured goods to such an extent that it was more profitable to export raw rather than finished materials, even in the case of silk where the northern Italian climate gave producers a huge natural advantage. Another factor, which related to Italy's 'passive revolution' and was referred to in many Marxist accounts as an explanation for slow economic growth, was the relative absence in Italy of capitalist entrepreneurs. There were, it was argued, few groups in Italy prepared to risk their savings in industrial ventures, new technology or other forms of speculative activity. Instead, merchants throughout Italy tended to invest in land, the traditional source of feudal power and status.

Rural landowners were also blamed for the condition of Italian agriculture, the backwardness of which was often taken for granted. Sereni's arguments about the persistence of feudal relations in southern agriculture fitted pre-existing notions of southern landowners as lazy, corrupt and unresponsive to market pressures. The development of commercial agriculture in Lombardy, arguably the most capitalist region in Italy, was seen to be equally hampered by absentee landowners and by complex share-cropping contracts that tied peasants to the land.[6] It could also be argued that similar contractual arrangements (the *mezzadria*) restricted peasant mobility in Tuscany, thereby maintaining low levels of consumption and preventing more rapid economic growth in the region.

This image of nineteenth-century Italy as an economically backward, late-industrialising nation, held back by rural society, passive revolution and the lack of capital or capitalists, is a powerful one. It is in part a legacy of Risorgimento rhetoric, and shares with the Risorgimento the perception of national decline and disappointment, as well as a search for those who are to blame. Nevertheless, as a means of understanding economic change during the period, this image is in many ways quite misleading, and has come under intense scrutiny and criticism in the last few years. Industrialisation and the South, the two areas of the Italian economy most associated with economic backwardness, have been the focus of much revisionist research. As a result, a very different, and considerably more positive, picture of industrial development and of southern economic life has emerged. At the same time, as we shall see, the new research has also led many historians to question the links between economics and Risorgimento, and to argue that nationalist ideas had little relevance for the economic activity of most Italians.

Proto-industrialistion and agriculture

The model of 'proto-industrialisation' describes and attempts to explain the process, widespread in Europe from the mid-seventeenth to the mid-nineteenth century, whereby industry became established in the countryside and employed the labour of peasant families on a part-time basis. Proto-industrial activity became particularly important in areas of poor agriculture, where peasants were able to use their wages from manufacturing to supplement their meagre incomes from the land. Proto-industrialisation differed from 'cottage' type industry in that goods were produced for distant, sometimes overseas, markets. Thus, the model describes a first stage of industrialisation; a mid-point between cottage and factory production. Historians of proto-industrialisation are, however, anxious to stress that the growth of proto-industry was in itself no guarantee of full industrialisation along factory lines, since areas of proto-industrial activity could just as easily fail to develop to the next stage, leading to a process of de-industrialisation. Although based on analyses of northern Europe (Saxony in particular), this model seemed to offer new possibilities for studying industrial development in Italy.

The proto-industrialisation model shares with previous models of industrialisation an emphasis on distinct stages in the evolution to full factory production. Yet it suggests, and allows for, far greater complexities in the industrialisation process. As a result, the peculiarities of Italy's economic experiences in the Risorgimento no longer seem quite so peculiar. The model seems particularly relevant in explaining the de-industrialisation experienced in the textile regions of the Centre and South, but it fits the emergence of successful textile industries in Lombardy and elsewhere equally well. It can also, arguably, explain the development of the entire northern Italian hill zone in this period.[7]

The applicability of the model of proto-industrialisation to northern Italy suggests that the region's reputation as a 'late-industrialiser' is a distortion. However, some historians of Italy have criticised the model for its assumption that proto-industrialisation can lead only to mass production or to de-industrialisation, suggesting instead far greater forms of variety and diversity. Focusing on the Brianza region of Lombardy, Anna Bull shows that the proto-industrialisation model cannot explain the successful emergence there of areas of small-scale industrialisation, rather than areas of mass production.[8] Giorgio Mori argues that a model of *pluriattività*, which describes the involvement of peasant families in multiple non-agricultural activities (for example, straw plaiting, mining or weaving) rather than a single proto-industrial activity, is more applicable to many parts of Italy. It was this pattern of industrial activity which lay behind the diffuse, gradual and uneven process of industrialisation experienced in nineteenth-century Italy. Far from being evidence of economic 'immobilism' and resistance to technological innovation, this kind of diversified, small-scale, rural production was an effective response to fluctuating world markets; it enabled entrepreneurs to adapt rapidly to changing market conditions, and to take advantage of cheap labour and readily accessible raw materials.[9]

An alternative view of labour and class relations, and of their role in the process of economic growth, has also emerged. For instance, the research of Franco Ramella and Anna Bull shows that the rural labour force was sometimes able to resist the exploitative pressures of entrepreneurs and carve out an independent position for itself. Their research challenges both the Marxist and the proto-industrialisation accounts of the social consequences of industrialisation: that is, they question the assumption that industrialisation led inevitably to the proletarianisation of the labour force. Bull argues instead that there existed a sexual division of labour within many peasant families, where the male head of the family exploited the labour of women to considerable personal profit. Where successful, this process could lead to capital accumulation and thus to small-scale ('diffused') entrepreneurship and profit, at least for the male heads of families.[10]

Research by Franco Bonelli and Luciano Cafagna broadens our perception of economic growth by questioning the central role played in it by industrialisation. Their model describes the accumulation of a surplus from agriculture over a long time-period, derived from trade and specifically from the export of primary products such as silk and cheese. The agricultural surplus provided the impetus for what Cafagna calls a 'pre-industrial' transformation of the northern Italian economy, which took place after 1820, possessed diffuse, proto-industrial characteristics and was based on artisan production. Only much later (during the 1890s), was there a second wave of industrialisation experienced in northern Italy, which was characterised by more concentrated factory production, increased mechanisation and rapid urbanisation. Both historians stress the gradualism of Italy's industrialisation; they argue that industrialisation should be depicted as a series of 'waves' rather than a single 'big spurt' or 'take-off'.[11]

If Italian economic growth is associated with changes in agriculture, then it becomes impossible to ignore the crucial role played by silk cultivators and silk merchants. Cafagna writes of an 'industrial–agricultural equilibrium' and of a 'happy relationship' (*un felice rapporto*) between industry and agriculture, which promoted economic growth in the region. It was through silk exports that northern Italy became integrated into world markets and its economy was transformed. The revenue generated from the exports of raw and spun silk, particularly in the early nineteenth century when world demand for textiles expanded at an enormous pace, provided the impetus for the development of banks and credit institutions, stimulated commercial involvement in industry, underlay the favourable balance of trade enjoyed by Italy until the 1880s and, finally, broadened the liberal political agenda to include a discussion of economic interests.[12] Agricultural exports provided the basis for economic growth inside Italy.

As a result of this reassessment of the importance of agriculture, low levels of internal demand which permitted a balance-of-payments surplus are seen as a positive advantage and not as a drag on economic growth. In the same way, the continuing (but actually never exclusive) tendency on the part of entrepreneurs and merchants to invest in land, or to locate industrial production in the countryside, is seen in a much more positive light. If agriculture was the power-house of the Italian economy, then investment in land was more a sign of entrepreneurial rationality than an indication of backward-looking attitudes.[13]

The 'Bonelli–Cafagna' model of Italian economic development represents an amalgam of various different models, incorporating elements from Sereni and Romeo, from the proto-industrialisation model and from Sidney Pollard's analysis of international trade as a transmitter of industrial technology.[14] Bonelli offers an account of the emergence of capitalism that is multi-causal and attempts to avoid the teleological pitfalls of Romeo's and Sereni's models. He uses a variety of different factors (market structure; the balance of payments; the availability of labour and capital) to explain economic growth in Italy, and he describes economic growth as an open-ended process which did not necessarily lead to industrialisation or a rapid economic 'take-off'. The integral part played by agricultural production in the economic transformation of northern Italy is no longer seen as dysfunctional, but as self-evident in explaining the particular pace and character of economic growth. In short, this assessment of Italy's economic performance in the nineteenth century challenges the categories of backwardness, and specifically those relating to the backwardness of agriculture.

One final feature of the Bonelli–Cafagna model – its marked emphasis on regions – is worth commenting on. Both Bonelli and Cafagna stress the strong regional variations in patterns of economic growth and analyse the integration of the northern Italian economy as a region into world markets. In part this reflects a general trend in economic analysis to focus on the crucial role played by regions, and not nations, in the construction of world markets. In a sense, therefore, and in noticeable contrast to previous accounts, this model makes no claim to describe or explain the economic differences within Italy. Economic dualism is simply taken as a pre-existing given; for Cafagna, 'the development of the North [in the first wave of industrialisation] was in no way conditioned by the existence of a backward South'.[15] This view is echoed by Giorgio Mori, who describes Italy's pre-unification economies as 'well and truly distinct', with conflicting interests and far greater trading links with non-Italian states than with each other.[16] There was no economic logic behind political unification, so economic growth and the development of unitarian nationalism in Italy must be seen as entirely distinct processes.

North and South

The analytical dissolution of the Italian economy into distinct regions, pursuing different kinds of economic development, has far-reaching implications. On the one hand, the Bonelli–Cafagna model, with its emphasis on silk production as the engine of economic growth in northern Italy, seems to imply a southern economy left out of the export-led expansion experienced in the

North. On the other hand, its insistence on the plurality of paths to economic growth suggests that the southern economy may merely have been following a separate developmental logic of its own.

In recent approaches to the South (or *Mezzogiorno*), much emphasis has been placed on different experiences of economic growth. It should be remembered that some southern industries were able to benefit from the Bourbon government's protectionist policies. A modern metallurgical industry developed in and around Naples before 1860, which suggests how rapidly certain sectors could expand, if protected from foreign competition by high tariff barriers.[17] For similar reasons, areas of textile production in the South experienced a notable process of technological modernisation and expansion in the early nineteenth century. Thus, the picture of uniform backwardness has to be modified: not all industry in the South was in decline, and not all sectors experienced a process of de-industrialisation.

The reassessment of Southern industry has been accompanied by a growing interest in the economies of the major ports, particularly the Sicilian ports. In Palermo, Messina and Trapani the volume of trade increased rapidly in this period, largely due to an expansion in the export of agricultural and other primary products.[18] A substantial merchant-shipping sector developed in Trapani in the early nineteenth century, suggesting a local economy capable of innovation and adaptation. The presence, in large numbers, of foreign (British, German) merchants and entrepreneurs in the commercial and industrial centres of the South is well known, and is often taken as evidence for a continuing lack of 'entrepreneurial spirit' among the southern middle classes. However, many Sicilian merchants (most obviously the Florio family) were involved in numerous and varied enterprises by the middle of the nineteenth century.[19] Arguably, it was only the greater visibility of these foreign entrepreneurs (most famously the Whitakers, Inghams and Woodhouses in Sicily) that obscured the equally important activities of their local counterparts.

It is with regard to Southern agriculture that most revisionist research has been carried out. The new direction taken by this research challenges a long, and distinguished, historiographical tradition which attributed Southern backwardness to the failure to change and innovate, a failure epitomised by the stagnant condition of its agriculture. From the eighteenth century onwards, writers argued that the 'immobility' of southern agriculture was the source of the country's backwardness, and that economic development in the South was hampered by the archaic attitudes and traditional practices associated with a rural, feudal past. This economic analysis also promoted a powerful political argument, suggesting that economic immobilism both benefited the particular economic interests and preserved the political privileges of the southern landowning class. 'War against the Latifondo', or government intervention in the shape of substantial political and economic reform, was seen as the appropriate solution.[20]

This economic and political orthodoxy has been challenged by an innovative group of southern historians. Piero Bevilacqua has stressed the importance of looking beyond feudalism, and of examining the impact of territorial and environmental changes on southern agriculture. Seen from this perspective, southern agriculture was not stagnant at all, but was undergoing a process of profound transformation due to the pressure of population on land.[21] Equally, the existence within the South of commercial and dynamic agricultural sectors, alongside more traditional areas, is given a far greater significance than before. Therefore, rather than being isolated exceptions to a pattern of economic immobility, the commercialised agriculture of the Terra di Lavoro near Naples, the Conca d'Oro of Palermo or the province of Puglia now tends to be seen within the context of more generalised change and economic complexity. Arguably, it is the sheer variety of forms of production, types of property and contract, degrees of soil fertility and patterns of demographic settlement, observable both within and between southern provinces, which is the single most striking characteristic of southern agriculture. And the most important distinction is between the dynamic export-led areas and those linked to production for self-sufficiency. Thus, every southern province had its own 'South': its own 'dualisms' between backward and dynamic sectors.[22]

Perhaps inevitably, revisions of this kind have also led historians to look again at the system of land holding in the South, and reassess hitherto established interpretations of the southern *latifondo*. These extensive grain-producing estates have long been held responsible for a host of southern ills: from desertification to malaria, from social injustice, peasant ignorance and popular violence to landlord absenteeism and cultural stagnation. in 1840, the historian Simonde de Sismondi described the *latifondo* as a collection of vast, vacant lands 'not cheered by the presence of a house, or of a dweller born and bred there, or of any sign of people's love for their native soil; in short, not gladdened by man's works.'[23] Some forty years earlier, a French traveller remarked that 'Europe ends at Naples and ends there quite badly. Calabria, Sicily, all the rest belongs to Africa'. These and similar views helped construct an idea of a land both abandoned by civilisation and caught in the grip of an atavistic past.[24]

To this long and illustrious tradition of research ('southernism' or *meridionalismo*), the work of Marta Petrusewicz has posed a major challenge. Basing her arguments on detailed research into the private archives of the Baracco estates in Calabria, she suggests that the latifundist estates of the nineteenth century were not so much a legacy of the past as the product of reform and revolution: specifically, they were a response to, and in part the creation of, the abolition of feudalism at the end of the eighteenth century and the development of capitalism in the countryside during the nineteenth. In parts of the Sicilian countryside too, a consolidation of landed estates took place in the first half of the nineteenth century, as middle-class landowners took advantage of government reforms and the indebtedness of the nobility to acquire ever-larger land holdings. Thus, the *latifondo*'s appearance of longevity and tradition is in fact quite misleading, and the extensive southern grain-estates should more accurately be considered an invention of modernity.

Moreover, instead of economic stagnation and resistance to innovation, Petrusewicz finds in the latifundist system:

a remarkable flexibility, which is manifested in the plurality of contractual associations, the variety of judicial institutions, a remarkable degree of crop diversification and the coexistence and interdependence of production for direct consumption and for the market.[25]

Through the balance between cash crops and self-sufficiency, the southern estates were able, at least until the agricultural depression of the 1880s, to adapt rapidly and effectively to changing market conditions. Perhaps even more importantly, the existence of an internal market provided by the peasants and the self-sufficiency of these estates meant that the welfare of peasants was guaranteed. Far from being exploitative of the peasant workforce, these large estates provided a kind of safety-net against proletarianisation or destitution.

All these revisions to the traditional picture of Southern backwardness have been controversial. The publication of Petrusewicz's *Latifondo* provoked a lively debate; some argued that she had greatly overestimated the efficiency and paternalism of the latifundist system,[26] others that she had overestimated the capacity of a 'few isolated valleys' of commercial development to transform the Southern economy.[27] Nevertheless, Petrusewicz's challenge to the idea of a single, monolithic and undeveloped Mezzogiorno has been profoundly influential. It has helped to generate a new generation of research on the South which refuses to take the categories of economic backwardness and stagnation as a given. In some cases, it has led scholars to question the notion of a 'Southern Question' as an ideological construction, linked more to the political struggles of unification and its long aftermath than to the economic and social realities of the region.[28]

If the revisionists are right, and the southern *latifondo* must be considered a rational variation on a capitalist theme, then how should we explain the absence of a more general process of economic growth in the South? Petrusewicz attributes the economic decline of the *latifondo* to the severe agrarian crisis of the 1880s when, she argues, the system was unable to adapt to the loss of overseas markets and the fall in grain prices. More generally, the weak political position of southern Italy both before and after unification probably hindered the ability of its merchants and entrepreneurs to improve their terms of trade with northern Europe.[29] Perhaps equally important was the impact of environmental change and, in particular, the growing land hunger caused by population increase and poor agricultural practices that upset the traditional balance between arable farming and pasture. The increasing percentage of land given over to arable farming, and the production of corn for export, entailed a far greater vulnerability to fluctuating world markets. The problems caused by an entirely inadequate infrastructure, especially the absence of a modern road network, also played a role in hampering economic growth, as did the failure to solve the chronic water shortage and establish an efficient irrigation system.[30]

Towards unification?

Some readers may wonder about the relevance of these debates to the Risorgimento and Italian unification. If so, they will have grasped the central argument of this chapter. The basic thrust of all these explanations, whether the Bonelli–Cafagna model of export-led expansion in the North or the stress on environment as a factor hampering southern agriculture, is to deny the existence of any straightforward relationship between political developments and economic growth. They challenge the link between economic change and political unification that has been fundamental to the historical agenda in Italy.

In these analyses, nationalism and the drive to political unification seem at best an irrelevance to, and at worst a diversion from, Italy's underlying economic problems. Many of the causes of Southern 'backwardness' more recently identified by historians – the vulnerability to fluctuating world markets, land hunger, the failure to irrigate – were never major political issues in the Risorgimento period. Probably the most important question for all the Italian economies in the nineteenth century was their integration into world markets, and here nationalism threw up obstacles rather than solutions. Different regions of Italy had different economies, with different export products and needs, and these were not helped by nationalist arguments in favour of a uniform Italian market.

It could be argued that the only characteristic shared by the Italian economies was a position of relative weakness *vis-à-vis* the core industrialising regions in Britain, France and Germany. The very advantages that cheap labour and low levels of internal demand offered to the Italian producer also proved, in the long run, to be disadvantages. The persistence of a low-wage economy may have greatly assisted exports but it also meant that there were few incentives for producers to develop or use new technologies, while the lack of internal markets for high-technology products was an additional constraint.[31] The attempt, made after national unification, to create national markets probably also damaged Italy's regional economies. On the one hand, the rapid imposition of a national economic policy linked to free trade dealt a damaging blow to southern industries. On the other hand, and over the longer term, the absence of Italian markets for Lombard silk or for Sicilian citrus fruits meant that these producers were very exposed to the rapid fluctuations of world markets.

Revisionist accounts of Italian economic development in the nineteenth century may ignore the Risorgimento, but these analyses have profound implications for our understanding of Risorgimento politics. They suggest that the liberal critique of the economic policies of Restoration governments was mistaken. The protectionist policies pursued by most governments were not unpopular, and they seem to have benefited rather than harmed many sectors of the economy. Nor was Restoration Italy lacking in economic success stories. Lombardy was a centre of export-led agricultural expansion; the Grand Duchy of Tuscany steered a 'middle way' which balanced economic conservatism in agriculture with speculation and innovation in the financial sector; and the Kingdom of the Two Sicilies presents a mixed picture of dynamic export sectors and traditional rural economies. Furthermore, if trade between regions and with world markets was the engine of economic expansion, then there was very little that these governments could usefully have done to promote economic growth or to cure economic 'backwardness'. Implicitly, therefore, revisionists also downplay the achievements of liberal administrations, and most notably the Cavourian administration, in attracting foreign investment, pursuing a free-trade policy and in encouraging economic growth. Here Cavour's success was considerable, but it was also unusual and appropriate only to the export-led economies of northern Italy. It could not provide the key to resolving all the problems and necessities of Italy's varied economies.[32]

In this way, the revisionist approach to Italian economic history links up with the revisionist approach to Restoration government and to Italian society. All these revisions stress the absence of any national framework, focusing on the local and regional context of economic activity and/or on its link to broader, international trends. Moreover, along with the focus on the regional and international constraints to political and economic change, the newer historiography shares a tendency to break down the old, Risorgimento distinctions between progress and reaction. Whether dealing with political demands, social unrest or economic development, the Restoration governments were never faced with a simple choice between tradition and modernity. Instead, the problem was one of reconciling diverse, and overlapping, local, regional, economic and political interests, without any means of adequately representing them within the administration. The failure of governments to formulate coherent economic policies was at least partly the result of the complex nature of the Italian economies.

Hence, the idea of a united Italy was a political idea with little economic resonance. The economic arguments made by Risorgimento liberals in favour of national unification were, according to most economic historians, the result of wishful thinking. Giorgio Mori states flatly that 'Prince Metternich was not wrong to observe that "Italy is a geographical expression"', and Mori attributes the demands for national unity not to any kind of economic logic but to what he calls the 'self-conscious and unrelenting drive from minority groups of intellectuals' to create an Italian nation state.[33] Such an objective, he argues, did not figure in the plans of the larger and more representative economic groups in Italy at this time, and still less did it figure in the aspirations of the urban and rural poor. According to Luciano Cafagna, the establishment of political unity may even have been an economic mistake, which retarded rather than promoted industrialisation. The idea that national unification could have caused the economic disparities between North and South is seen as a fiction, a fiction that derived from political pressures and internal struggles for political supremacy.[34]

So why did national unification take place? How were these unrepresentative, 'minority groups of intellectuals' able to establish an Italian nation state in 1860? It is already apparent, from chapter 3, that Italian liberals offered little in the way of a radical or coher-

6

Nation, Identity and Nationalist Politics

Nationalism and historiography

Nationalist politics were always the central concern in the history of the Risorgimento. For at least a hundred years after unification, their primacy was taken for granted, and the political struggles of the Risorgimento were examined in depth long before economic development or social structure became legitimate historical concerns. Studies of personality determined the initial direction of Risorgimento history, and its sources were the personal reminiscences of prominent liberals and biographical writing about them.[1] In the broader political formula (discussed in the next chapter) whereby the Risorgimento was recast as a 'foundation story' for the new Kingdom of Italy, its leaders were united after death to become the subject of extended personality cults. Historians ranked Cavour, Mazzini, Vittorio Emanuele II and, above all, Garibaldi among the 'Great Men' of the Italian nation; they had restored Italian genius and were leading supporters of liberty, economic progress, monarchical loyalty and national heroism. As a result of its political unification, Italy also seemed proof of the link between nationalism and nation-state formation. Its existence appeared to be striking confirmation of nationalist claims that national communities were the legitimate and inevitable basis for modern polities and were merely waiting to be liberated or restored by the right political leaders. Thus, the hegemony of nationalism had part of its basis in historical writing and found its way into post-unification interpretations of the Risorgimento.

Detailed historical research, inspired in part by a sense of disillusionment with the outcome of the Risorgimento, has long since dented the heroic myths of nationalist historiography. In fact, soon after Italian unification, some historians of diplomacy identified Cavour, along with the Prussian leader Otto von Bismarck, as the representative of a new 'realist', or pragmatic and self-interested, approach to politics. For these historians, Cavour represented a new breed of modern politician, a creator of *Realpolitik*: discarding accepted rules of diplomacy and aiming simply to manipulate the international situation and maximise nationalist aspirations for his own political advantage.[2] Much later, during the 1950s and early 1960s, a new realist orthodoxy emerged in Risorgimento history, which rejected completely the glorious mythologies so dear to Italian nationalists. Denis Mack Smith may have challenged traditional accounts of Cavour's 'realism', but he did so to argue that the leader was inept and inconsistent, and he confirmed the cynical assessment of his personality and aims. Mack Smith's book on the relationship between Cavour and Garibaldi in 1860 has the revealing subtitle *A Study in Political Conflict*.[3] For Mack Smith, and other historians influenced by his work, the creation of a united Italy in 1861 reflected the political rivalries rather than the nationalist aspirations of the Risorgimento period. The role of nationalism as a cause of political unification was played down, if not excluded entirely. Far from being the culmination of the Risorgimento, the wars of 1859–60 came to be seen as an example of state-making and state-breaking, the work of ambitious politicians who cared little, if at all, about the freedom of so-called nations.

The non-nationalist direction taken by political historians of the Risorgimento from the 1950s onwards reflected wider post-war anxieties about nationalism and its role in European politics. Few historians followed the approach to the history of ideas outlined by Federico Chabod and Adolfo Omodeo in the last years of fascism and war.[4] Instead, most became less interested in political ideas *per se* and began to concentrate more on party politics and political behaviour, and on strictly empirical research. They also relied on a very different set of sources. Here the impetus was the opening of archives and the publication of many primary sources, notably Cavour's voluminous correspondence. Historical attention became focused on the analysis of dynastic (Piedmontese) aims, political expediency and international rivalry in the making of Italian unity, or on what could be uncovered from official documents and political letters and diaries. Inspired in part by the availability of so much new primary material, many liberal historians turned to the study of minor characters and lesser-known episodes; they implicitly rejected the 'grand narrative' of nationalism, even as they condemned Mack Smith's negative judgement on the Risorgimento.[5]

Further to the left, a new political history developed which challenged Italy's foundation story in its entirety. It emphasised the bitter divisions in the liberal-nationalist movement, especially the rivalries between moderate liberals and Mazzinians, and the elements of conflict within the Mazzinian movement itself. Much greater significance was given to Mazzini's refusal to endorse a federalist and/or socialist programme and to the gradual defeat of his movement during the 1850s. This period was no longer considered as the culmination of nationalist ambitions, but seen instead as the moment at which the Mazzinians became divided, were sidelined by Cavour and the liberal moderates and lost much of their support among the middle classes.[6] In these analyses, nationalism tended to be treated in terms of party politics and political conflict, while its heroic legends and protagonists were regarded with suspicion.[7]

The establishment of a non-political, Marxist–Gramscian, approach to the Risorgimento, which stressed the impact of long-term economic and social change on Risorgimento politics, also confirmed the negative assessment of Italian unification and the tendency to relegate the role of nationalism. Risorgimento nationalism was increasingly seen as a movement of (primarily urban, middle-class) elites, with no interest in the poorer members of society and no basis for establishing support in the countryside. As we have seen in the course of this book, unification was explained mainly as the reflection of a broader process of change, of a 'dual' economic and political revolution that saw the rise of industrial capitalism and the growth of nation states. The problems of unification, in turn, were attributed to the weakness of the middle class and its revolution, and correspondingly to the leadership's inability to impose its liberal-nationalist vision on Italian culture. In all this research, a consensus on Italy as a 'weak', 'failed' or 'peculiar' nation was consolidated.

During the 1980s, finally, a new or revisionist approach emerged which disagreed with the nationalist, realist and Marxist explanations of Italian unification and sought to shift attention entirely away from the Risorgimento. Revisionists were virtually unanimous in rejecting (indeed, ignoring) the nationalist explanation of unification, pointing both to the persistence of regional and local identities and/or conflicts in Risorgimento Italy and to the stability and logic of Restoration government. They treated the realist explanation with suspicion, disliking its focus on high politics, and associating it especially with a sense of Italy's failure to live up to a hypothetical, and non-existent, Anglo-Saxon norm. They also took issue with the Marxist assumption of a single, developmental logic between the rise of capitalism, the growth of a middle class and the political unification of Italy, although they followed Marxist historians in privileging social and economic explanation over political analysis. Relying on social and economic records, on bureaucratic and police papers, and above all on research in regional, local and family archives, they constructed a new history for early nineteenth-century Italy. What emerged was a rich, varied and complex picture of changing societies, whose politics and identities were unaffected by any notion of the national.

As we have seen in previous chapters, the implications of this revisionist approach are important and far-reaching. The dissatisfaction with existing explanations of Italian unification manifests itself most clearly in a denial of the obviousness and significance of nationalism itself. Instead, revisionist historians stress the continuity between the political struggles of Restoration and liberal Italy, a continuity that can be attributed to the continuing, and unresolved, pressures of economic and political modernisation. Much of the social instability of the period, they argue, was local or regional in character, and could even be based on interpersonal rivalries between families. There was no single Italian society or economy, but a huge variety of different groups and interests: some dynamic, some stagnant and some a mixture of both. Very few of them were struggling towards greater self-realisation as part of a single, Italian nation.

At the same time, research seemed to show that the persistent instability of nineteenth-century Italian politics could be more accurately attributed to a vigorous resistance to change, notably to the centralisation of political institutions and the threat to traditional local identities, rather than to an unsatisfied desire for national unification. Finally, during the late 1980s and especially after the fall of communism in 1989, interpretative categories such as 'moderatism', 'Jacobinism' and 'democracy', used by Marxist historians to explain and analyse the political changes of the Risorgimento, were recontextualised and substantially challenged.[8] The combined effect was to break down all previous narratives – critical as well as favourable – of the process of Italian unification.

National unification was reinterpreted as the 'meeting of ruling classes with different political traditions.'[9] It was, according to Giovanni Sabbatucci and Vittorio Vidotto, 'the fortunate result of a complex mix of factual circumstances and individual choices' rather than the result of an inexorable national logic; and it represented 'a real break, an undeniable qualitative leap with respect to the prevailing tendencies and developments' of early nineteenth-century Italy. In short, revisionists stress the 'accidental character'[10] of national unification, and see it as only one possible outcome among many.

The merits of this approach in enriching our understanding of nineteenth-century Italy are undeniable. But perhaps its most interesting consequence was entirely unintended. By burying once and for all the grand narrative of nationalism as the origin of the Italian nation-state, as well as undermining the various realist and Marxist counter-narratives, revisionist historians indirectly revitalised the debate on national identity. For if the political odds were so obviously stacked against them, how and why did opposition elites struggle to create a united Italy?[11] How, in an Italy characterised by municipal interests, traditional loyalties and separate economies, did the nationalists win the argument against Restoration rulers? How was resistance to change transformed into the appearance of a consensus in its favour? Moreover, if Italy was oblivious to nationalist sentiment, how can the fame and popularity of Garibaldi be explained? And why did Cavour perceive an advantage in manipulating nationalist opinion? Finally, if there was no economic or political logic to national unification, what made it happen? It is by bringing these questions to the fore that the revisionist concern with the local and regional, its rejection of any single, national path to modernisation and its rehabilitation of Restoration government, has reopened the debate on Italian culture and brought politics back to the centre of the story.

The culture of the nation

One of the starting points of recent research is a re-evaluation of the roots of Italian nationalism. Thus, even if a political Italy did not exist before the middle of the nineteenth century, it seems clear that a strong and growing sense of cultural 'Italian-ness' (*italianità*) prevailed among a small educated elite long before. Culture, and not politics or economics, was the real sign of Italian identity. In the eighteenth century, this identity was expressed in the intellectual interests and associational life of elites throughout the peninsula, and in their language, literature, music and visual arts, and it was further shaped by the presence of the Catholic Church and by opposition to it. In Enlightenment thinking, moreover, the meaning of the word 'nation' came to be identified not just with 'birthplace' and a shared territory but also with this Italian cultural community which possessed a common language and literature.

This culture was, in turn, stimulated by the French invasions and occupations of Italy between 1796 and 1815. During the short-lived Republics (1797–99), the Jacobins introduced new symbols and rituals and, most of all, they were responsible for the arrival of a new political vocabulary of revolution which the older language of *italianità* absorbed, manipulated and transposed onto itself. Thenceforth, the iconography of the Italian nation and its concepts of patriotism and citizenship were modelled on those of the French Republic, but, at the same time, the culture continued to refer to traditional elements of *italianità* like geography, language and religion.[12]

Although the revolutionary period was followed by a political backlash, and Restoration rulers sought not only to punish those who had supported the Revolution but also to repress revolutionary symbols, rituals and language through the use of censorship, by and large they failed to notice and/or control the growing popularity of the idea of Italy in the arts: in poetry, novels, opera, histories and painting. The idea of Italy – its past, places and protagonists – was given additional force in the early Restoration period by the arrival of the romantic movement, somewhat later in Italy than in northern Europe but with a correspondingly less conservative bent and with a broader popular reach. Romanticism in Italy incorporated a strong religious sensibility with progressive eighteenth-century ideas. Italian romantics were both cosmopolitan and national-minded: they united around what they called the 'modernisation' of Italian literature and society, looking at northern European countries as their models, but they did so while celebrating their own history and culture. They spoke of the need for art and literature to reach the 'people' and of a distinguished literary, linguistic and artistic tradition which was specifically 'Southern' and had its roots in a 'national' past.

The idea of the nation in Risorgimento Italy was based on a fusion of all these different elements. An existing culture of secular and religious *italianità*, the vocabulary of French patriotism and the language of Romanticism (itself a mixture of tradition and modernity) defined the belief in, and enthusiasm for, the nation in early Restoration Italy. Drawing for the first time not on official documents and correspondence but on a rich variety of literary and visual sources, notably the novels, poems, paintings and histories of the period, Alberto Banti has advanced a different interpretation of the origins and growth of Italian national identity. He has identified what he calls a 'Risorgimento canon', that is, some forty texts through which, as he puts it, the future young patriots of Italy 'discover' the nation, and 'understand that it is necessary to fight for her'.[13] Through the work of Romantic novelists like Alessandro Manzoni, Francesco Domenico Guerrazzi and Massimo d'Azeglio, as well as the poetry of Ugo Foscolo and Giacomo Leopardi, the operas of Gioachino Rossini, Vincenzo Bellini and Giuseppe Verdi and the paintings of Francesco Hayez, both patriots and the wider reading public 'discovered' a national community and a common past, with an appeal which was all the more potent because it was heard in novels, paintings and song.

For Banti, there is a single continuum which ties the images, metaphors and narratives of these texts to the national-patriotic discourse of Risorgimento politics. In Risorgimento texts and the political rhetoric of Italian nationalists the nation is imagined in similar ways: a voluntary pact amongst a free and equal fraternity; an organic community; an extended family; and a shared historical identity. In short, the nation is a community established by the bonds of affection, nature, kinship and history. Yet the nation is also under threat, and Italy's more recent past must be written as a story of decadence, foreign domination and internal division. Hence, a common theme of Risorgimento narratives and political rhetoric is suffering, danger, and repression – a hero betrayed, a woman dishonoured, a land oppressed by foreign tyranny – and with this threat comes an equal emphasis on the redemptive power of courage, rebellion and martyrdom, and an exaltation of individual and collective struggle in defence of the community.

Banti's approach to Italian national identity, first outlined in *La nazione del Risorgimento* (2000), has dramatically altered and revitalised historical debate on the Risorgimento. This seems to have been his conscious intention. 'One should not expect a traditional approach from this volume', is the opening sentence of a path-breaking collection of essays on the Risorgimento edited by Banti and Paul Ginsborg: 'because the idea of this collection is something else: to take a major step towards a different history of the Risorgimento'. Banti's model is also different. He is inspired by the new cultural history, and especially by the 'linguistic turn' of historical inquiry, which developed in the late 1980s and the 1990s; his analysis is driven more by the search for meaning and experience than it is by the more conventional historical questions of causality and change over time. The aim, to quote Banti and Ginsborg again, is 'to bring the deep culture of the Risorgimento to life, to observe the mentalities, the feelings, the emotions, the life trajectories, the political and personal projects of the men and women who took part in the Risorgimento.'[14]

This focus on culture leads Banti, and other proponents of the same approach, to reassess the significance of nationalism and of the Risorgimento. First, it is possible to take issue with the now commonplace idea of a fractured national identity, weakened by conflicts between moderate liberals and democrats. Instead, as Banti argues, there was 'a kind of coherent narrative of the Italian nation ... a sort of *single way of thinking* the nation' which relied on a common set of themes, tropes and symbols.[15] Or, as Silvana Patriarca puts it: 'patriots of different stripes shared common sentiments and cultural conceptions about that obscure object of desire, the nation, starting with the common use of the very words "Risorgimento" and "regeneration" to indicate the enterprise in which they were involved and their common aspiration.'[16]

Moreover, the attention to culture – as opposed to social structure or high politics, and the treatment of culture as a variable independent of both – leads to a crucial reappraisal of Italian nationalism's reach and importance. The Risorgimento, according to Banti and Ginsborg, 'was a "mass" movement'. It involved the active participation of tens of thousands of people in its wars, political struggles, festivals and commemorations, and it was observed by, written about and affected many more.[17] Equally, by reminding us of the role of Romanticism in creating the idea of the nation, Ginsborg has emphasised the significance of the Risorgimento as part of a much larger European cultural movement.[18]

In turn, the Risorgimento contributed to the elaboration of a Romantic 'moment' in nineteenth-century politics. Spread in part by the experience and myth of political exile, and by the creation of a diasporic network, the cause of Italian freedom acquired a meaning not just for Italians but also outside Italy as part of a 'Liberal International' movement.[19] The Risorgimento had an impact on British, French, and other European and American cultures and on internal political allegiances. The growth of an international public opinion favourable to Italian nationalism also affected diplomatic decisions in the late 1850s, created a press frenzy around the events of Italian unification, and led many (perhaps thousands) of non-Italians to fight in the wars of 1859 and 1860. Far from being a minority movement of an isolated elite, the Risorgimento seems to have been of pivotal importance in the formation and diffusion across Europe of the ideas, rituals and practices of a new political identity.

This proposal of Italian nationalism as a potent and widely influential movement of culture is confirmed by extensive research. For example, attention to the culture – as opposed to the organisation and institutions – of the literary and artistic public sphere suggests that it was increasingly 'Italianised' in the years before Italian unification. That is, even as cultural activity remained a local affair based on regional networks and associations, its language, rituals, themes and subjects became more Italian. Italy was an especially strong presence in the visual and performing arts: in painting, music and plays (all areas of Italian culture until recently neglected by historians of the Risorgimento). Theatre in particular played a nationalising role. The popularity of opera led to a wave of theatre construction in major cities and small towns, and these theatres created a recognisable and uniform public architecture across the Italian peninsula.[20] The music itself was both a symbol of *italianità* and a critical vehicle for its popularisation. Romantic themes such as oppression, betrayal, struggle and redemption were diffused by melodramas which, with a simple and immediate sentimentality, 'told of passionate and unhappy love stories; the love of fatherland intensified by captivity and exile; the force of love against the forces of tradition and power; and the rebellion of youth doomed to defeat.'[21] During the 1840s and thereafter, a section of the liberal public seized on and publicised such music as an example of the growing patriotic spirit in Italy. Thus, both the theatres themselves and the performances in them provided and helped construct a sense of imagined community in Italy.[22]

The Italian language, once dismissed as a minority language used by few and appreciated by still fewer, has also undergone something of a scholarly rehabilitation. Italian was spoken with enthusiasm by the educated elite, understood by a much larger percentage of the population than was previously thought (10 per cent rather than 2 per cent),[23] and relied upon as a language of communication by many tourists in the peninsula. In some areas of cultural life, notably in the vibrant publishing sector of Milan and Florence where both entrepreneurs and writers had a vested interest in market expansion, there was a clear effort, and something of a trend, towards the establishment of a more national network with Italian interests which went beyond the local and regional. Equally, there was a growing national (if still middle-class) market for Risorgimento books in nineteenth-century Italy. There were, for instance, publishing 'crazes' for the novels of D'Azeglio and the poems of Foscolo, as well as for the political works of Gioberti and Balbo, and even for banned books such as General Pepe's memoirs.

Similar nationalising processes can be observed in intellectual activity, most notably in the growth of economic and scientific associations. From the 1830s onwards, liberal agrarian associations in the Restoration states began to seek contact with each other on a national scale. So, while the economies of Italy followed separate paths to economic modernisation, economic thought and the economists themselves became more explicitly Italian.

Indeed, the new science of economics, and especially the flourishing interest in economic theory and debates about economic growth among Italian liberals, helped consolidate a view of Italy as a living national community.[24] During the 1840s, a series of congresses were held in different cities in the Italian peninsula which gathered scientists together from all over Italy, and they addressed scientific questions in terms which assumed the existence of a national interest. An enthusiasm for statistical analysis among intellectual elites also reflected and helped shape the Italian nationalist discourse. In statistical research and publications, the peninsula was often considered as a whole, as if Italy was already a unified nation; as with economics, statistics helped to build a 'portrait' of the nation, and to legitimate the sense of an Italian national community as an existing, scientific reality.[25]

New research has also stressed the impact of Italian nationalism on private life and on women. On the one hand, during the Risorgimento and accentuated by the emergence of a new, stricter sexual morality in the course of the nineteenth century, the separation between the public and private spheres was confirmed and rigidified. Women were increasingly confined to private life and their patriotic duty was defined in terms of the family, and its promotion and care. On the other hand, some women did break through the confines of the private and became active in the politics and wars of the Risorgimento.

Moreover, both the public and private spheres were sustained by a series of inter-connecting networks and symbols. Family and/or friends provided crucial material and emotional support for Risorgimento patriots, especially those forced into exile and/or the underground,[26] while Risorgimento stories of love, honour, loss, struggle and salvation had not only a public expression but also an intense personal resonance. For many Risorgimento patriots, the idea of the nation as an extended family headed by a mother was part of a real, lived experience and above all of a culture which stressed the role of maternal love;[27] so that in terms of the relationship between the family and the outside world, there was a great deal of imaginative fluidity between the public and private spheres.[28] It is precisely in this nexus between public and private that Italian nationalism found its fervent emotional force. And it is in this wide, pervasive and diffuse appeal, rather than in immediate political results, that historians now seek the sources and contours of nationalism's political influence and assess the achievements of Risorgimento patriots.

These pioneering attempts to explore the links between family, civil society and the state have uncovered discontinuities and contradictions as well as connections and fluidity. Romantic aesthetics in Italy may have exalted motherly love but these ideals were not always reflected in affective relations within families. Nationalist beliefs identified national communities with the family, but families and lovers could be disrupted and torn apart by the new sense of national belonging. Family love and love of country could contradict each other and when they did, especially in relations between parents and children, passionate feelings and the emotional call of both were intensified. The patriot Aurelio Saffi could write to his English wife, Giorgina Craufurd, that 'the image of the fatherland and of yourself are permanently linked in my heart', but many nationalists who embraced the fatherland instead broke with their families, and then dedicated themselves entirely to politics and rarely formed new families of their own.[29]

For example, Massimo Taparelli d'Azeglio, moderate politician, painter, novelist and son-in-law of Alessandro Manzoni, may seem proof of the union between private life, cultural pursuits and political action, but in reality he strove to keep these spheres strictly separate from each other. His marriage to Giulietta Manzoni was a failure and, as moderate prime minister of Piedmont between 1849 and 1852, there was very little about his achievements which could be called romantic.[30] D'Azeglio also had a radically different political outlook from his brother Luigi, Jesuit priest and founding editor of *La Civiltà Cattolica*, and in this he was not unusual. The activities of the Neapolitan democrat Giuseppe Ricciardi were deplored by his pro-Bourbon brother Giulio and sister Elisabetta, even though Elisabetta helped him in exile and wrote him constant letters, while his other sister, Irene, sympathised with his political beliefs.[31]

In his memoirs, Giuseppe Garibaldi exalted the family and love between parent and child, husband and wife, and he enjoyed a private life of sorts. Yet it was highly unconventional for the time, and permeated by the political. His first wife, Anita, was a married woman when he eloped with her, and their first child was born out of wedlock. After her death, Garibaldi consistently pursued parallel sexual relationships with a variety of female companions, but without depending on any one of them long-term, at least until old age confined him to a bath chair at Caprera, for either company or happiness. Pursuit of his political and military career meant that he hardly saw his first three children as they grew up, and he seems to have been equally committed to his political 'brothers', men like Nino Bixio and Augusto Vecchi with whom he shared his remarkable public life. At the same time, his version of private life at Caprera provided one basis for political activity. Garibaldi's many lovers were all 'sisters', in that they shared his political ideas and helped promote the nationalist agenda, while Caprera served both as a 'backstage' – a place where Garibaldi could organise political campaigns unobserved – and as a more privileged platform where he and his companions could act out a narrative of domestic harmony.[32]

Arguably, it is in this exploration of the public and private, and of the individual experiences and relationships of men and women, that the new historiography of the Risorgimento can lay claim to real originality. It raises questions of methodology and interpretation which should prove of general interest to all historians of gender and politics. Still there are some gaps and problems in this new approach. At the current stage of research, the question of whether the Risorgimento can really be called a mass movement remains open. The connections between high and popular culture, and between secular and religious culture need further elucidation, and not enough is known about the relationship between cultural developments and social change, or between cultural forms of identification and political action. In sharp contrast to most other nineteenth-century nationalist movements, Italian patriots took little interest in rural life and folk culture, so it would be useful to know more about what, if any, impact this urban literate culture had on the rural illiterate poor. Religion still remains somewhat unrepresented in the new historiography: there are some interesting studies of the fusion of religious symbolism and language with the discourse of the nation, but far fewer which examine the Church's ideological and tactical response to the manipulation of its vocabulary by the nationalists.[33]

We may accept the argument that the Risorgimento was a mass movement in terms of its popularity among sections of the middle-class public and the enthusiasm with which many greeted the idea of the nation. But this re-evaluation should also encourage us to examine in much more detail how, and in what ways, the Risorgimento achieved popularity, and it should not lead us to ignore those who opposed the Risorgimento or were insensible to its appeal. We should, of course, recognise the innovative and essentially modern characteristics of the Risorgimento, especially its capacity to evoke an intense emotional response and create feelings of belonging and community among the liberal public. However, the paradigmatic shift involved in this re-evaluation – from society and class, to culture and the imaginary – could be more fully acknowledged, and its methodological implications need to be further explored. The question of causality (what caused national unification?) is not entirely resolved by the move to representations and meaning, however fruitful this latter analysis is proving to be. Even now, we know comparatively little about what happened to transform a vibrant cultural movement of nationalism into a clearly more compromised political programme.

The recent rehabilitation of Italian nationalism emphasises its emotional appeal, thereby placing great stress on the irrational and natural (or 'organic') elements of the nationalist discourse. One problem with this emphasis on emotions is that it can lead to a neglect of other, more rational elements, perhaps most notably the political ideas which became an integral part of the same discourse. Thus, the call for freedom, equality and/or democracy which drove nationalism as a political movement, and was an inspiration to generations of activists, can be treated as subordinate to emotional feelings of hate, vengeance and love.[34] The emphasis on emotions also raises questions about how historians should study feelings and emotional responses in the past. Moreover, by privileging cultural trends the new cultural approach risks reducing the political changes of mid-nineteenth-century Italy to a simple expression of nationalist opinion, and thus inadvertently reverting to the much older nationalist narrative described in the first section of this chapter. In the absence of any other explanation of political unification, the new historiography can seem implicitly to cast nationalism – the political awakening of Italy to a consciousness of itself – as the author and protagonist of institutional change.

One way forward is to separate analytically nationalism as a cultural movement from nationalism as a programme for political action, and to recognise that the link between culture and action was provided by political thought.[35] We should remember that nationalism as a political movement was the creation of opposition groups in Restoration Italy who also disagreed with each other, and that foremost among them were revolutionaries led by Giuseppe Mazzini, and moderate nationalists who despised Mazzini's politics. Both the Mazzininians and the moderates framed their struggle for political power in terms of the nation, combining an emotional appeal to national identity with a trenchant critique of Restoration ideology and government. They all absorbed or appropriated the nationalist discourse for political purposes; however, they also argued about political methods and outcomes and notably about the desirability of democracy and republicanism in Italy.

In this way, an analysis of the politics of national identity, or of political thought and action in the Risorgimento, is central to explaining the political changes of mid-century Italy. In what follows, I will outline some elements of a new approach to Risorgimento politics. My suggestion is that this approach can recognise the immense appeal of nationalism in Italian cultural life, but should also analyse its impact on the process of institutional change; above all, we must seek to explain the astonishing achievement of national unification, and the conflicts and reversals which surrounded it.

The politics of the nation

Giuseppe Mazzini was a typical product of the Risorgimento culture described above. In an exemplary autobiographical statement of romantic obsession with suffering, decadence and death (and we should also note the reference to his 'poor mother'), he described his discovery of romantic Italy as a moment of personal conversion and understanding. Inspired by an emotional reading of the Romantic canon – of Manzoni, Walter Scott, Simonde de Sismondi, Madame de Staël and, above all, Vittorio Alfieri and Ugo Foscolo – he identified his own youthful unhappiness with the pain of his 'fatherland':

> At the desks of the University . . . in the middle of the unruly mass of student life, I was gloomy, absorbed, and seemed like one suddenly grown old . . . I childishly decided to dress always in black, as a sign of mourning for my fatherland. The *Ortis* [*Ultime lettere di Jacobo Ortis* by Foscolo] fell into my hands and drove me mad: I learnt it by heart. Things got so out of hand that my poor mother worried I would commit suicide . . . We young men were all romantics.[36]

Yet Mazzini also rejected what he saw as the melancholy, passivity and nostalgia of Romanticism in favour of political rebellion. In a process which was to become characteristic of the scavenging tendencies of all nationalist strategy, he fused his cultural sensibilities with an eclectic mix of political and social ideas to develop the aims and methods of his movement. From the revolutionary Jacobins, some of whose principles he absorbed via the Italian Jacobin Filippo Buonarotti and the *carboneria* conspiracies of the 1820s, Mazzini borrowed a confidence in the transformative power of politics. From them he also developed a particular faith in political leadership and in small heroic groups of insurrectionaries, or even an individual, who could provide what he called a revolutionary 'spark' and lead the people towards a general revolutionary uprising. Like the Jacobins, he also conceived a new way of thinking, behaving and speaking politically and, like them, he sought to establish an entirely different political language for this Republic, with popular rituals and symbols of national belonging.

Mazzini was not just a Jacobin and he also defined his beliefs in opposition to them. He was equally inspired by the post-revolutionary Saint-Simonians, and especially by their more mystical and Catholic elements represented by the liberal priest, Felicité de Lamennais, and the Polish nationalist, Adam Mickiewicz. From them, he drew a belief in the creation of a new society based on the principles of progress, religious faith, association and a duty towards the national community rather than just individual rights. Particularly worthy of note was his borrowing of their vision of God and the role of the divine in history; and his famous motto 'God and the People' was of Saint-Simonian origin.[37] For Mazzini, God was the ultimate and real source of sovereignty, and he saw in the overthrow of the old political system of privilege – of the hierarchy of kings, clergy and nobility – the means of recasting the bond between the people (no longer mere individuals but united as a nation) and the divine.

Mazzini's innovation was to have incorporated a romantic idea of the nation with political activism and voluntarism, on the one hand, and with popular theocracy, on the other. He dismissed the broad assumption of French leadership in the revolutionary struggle and argued it was now Italy's mission to usher in the new age of nationalism. His ambition was the creation of a single, unitary Republic across the entire territory of Italy, based on the 'unity, independence [and] liberty' of its citizens and providing leadership for other aspirant nations.

To this end, Mazzini established in 1831 a revolutionary organisation which he called 'Young Italy'. 'Young Italy' was to be different from the revolutionary secret societies which preceded it by its refusal to rely only on conspiratorial methods and by its rejection of French leadership; it was based around youth because the young had no memory of the French Revolution and were instead the bearers of a new Romantic spirit and culture. Only they could carry out the task of quasi-religious 'resurrection' which Mazzini envisaged for Italy, and it was to the youth of Italy that he extended a personal and political model of utter dedication, ceaseless activity and individual sacrifice for the cause of Italian liberation.

Mazzini was, and remains, a controversial figure. 'Views of Mazzini tend to be extreme', comments one of his recent biographers; he was hugely admired in England, his land of exile, but both in Italy and in the European democratic movement 'rivals, opponents, and enemies may well have outnumbered support-ers'.[38] His insurrectionary methods and belief in a unitary Italian republic were denounced by contemporaries; for example, Young Italy was condemned by Massimo d'Azeglio as 'foolish', 'perverse' and 'useless'.[39] In the 1850s Mazzini lost much of his support after a series of failed insurrections and botched uprisings, which have led one English historian to dismiss him as a cynic who must bear his share of the responsibility for the failure of the democratic movement in Italy and the conservative turn of Italian (and European) politics from the late 1850s onwards.[40] Even those histo-rians who do not condemn him admit he is a difficult figure to judge: 'hard to classify ideologically and politically' with a life 'full of ironies and paradoxes', who 'worked on the minds of men rather than through the more easily studied means of politics, diplomacy or military conquest.'[41]

However, these criticisms seem somewhat to miss the point about Mazzini's contribution to political change. Above all, it is Mazzini who provides the link between nationalism as a cultural identity and nationalism as a political movement. Mazzini recog-nised that the most immediate obstacle facing revolutionary nationalists was a problem of credibility: not only, as we have seen in the course of this book, were there huge practical obstacles to the establishment of a unitary republic, but, the emotional appeal of cultural nationalism notwithstanding, there were also no obvious or unmistakable signs of people belonging to a national commu-nity. Mazzini's real achievement lay in his solution to the latter problem. His advance was not so much to organise Young Italy (which, in truth, resembled the failed secret societies that he so decried) but to exercise it as a tool of propaganda and to develop it as the centre for a much broader network of political influence and support. His success was to have seen that the key to making the Romantic idea of Italy political was through a process of commu-nication and that, in the post-revolutionary world, political victory lay as much in persuasion and symbolic action as it did in control of institutional power.

From the outset of his political career in the early 1830s, Mazzini evolved three related strategies for making the Romantic idea of

Italy politically convincing. The first of these was his use of the press. Before many of his contemporaries, Mazzini understood the critical role played by the printed word (newspapers, magazines, pamphlets, novels and memoirs) and pictures in producing a broad sense of imagined community. 'A newspaper must be an act of devotion [*sacerdozio*], a missionary work', he wrote in 1848. Already twelve years earlier he had described the press as 'a power':

> perhaps the only power in modern times. It is this power for the methods it uses, for the nature of its mission; because it speaks and insists . . . it speaks to all the classes; it discusses all questions; it touches all the cords which move in the human soul; it travels rapidly and when it speaks to a country establishes itself straightaway . . . it is for the intellect what steam is for industry.[42]

When he founded Young Italy in 1831, Mazzini simultaneously established a newspaper (*Giovine Italia*); and from exile in London after 1837, he soon published another one, the *Apostolato Popolare*, addressed directly 'To Italians and especially to Italian workers',[43] which he attempted to distribute around Britain and Europe and to smuggle into Italy. Its pages were filled with a mix of current affairs reporting, nationalist editorials written by himself, biographies of famous Italians, romantic poetry and reviews of novels and histories by writers like D'Azeglio, Guerrazzi and Michele Amari. *Apostolato Popolare* is proof of Mazzini's attempt to harness the popularity of Romantic culture, to direct its narrative themes and artistic forms to specifically political ends and to reach a very broad audience (including 'Italian workers').

Later in the 1840s, Mazzini relied on the press and publishing to produce perhaps his greatest publicity triumph – the creation and popularisation of Giuseppe Garibaldi, a young Italian soldier exiled in Uruguay, as the new Italian hero. He wrote about Garibaldi's exploits in *Apostolato Popolare* and in letters to the *Times* in London, he helped produce extensive articles on him in the underground press and he persuaded more moderate publishers like Lorenzo Valerio to write in praise of Garibaldi's selfless heroism upholding political liberty and Italian heroism in South

America. He even commissioned a portrait of Garibaldi ('it is worth promoting his fame', he commented), which was lithographed and circulated to raise money for the nationalist cause.[44] So successful was the Mazzinian propaganda around Garibaldi that, by the time the man himself returned to Italy in the spring of 1848, arriving just after the outbreak of revolution and in time for the war on Austria, he was already a celebrated figure, identified with a Romantic narrative of *italianità* and an explicit symbol of the political 'resurrection' which Mazzini promoted so tirelessly in his publications.[45]

Publishing and writing also helped to create an extended political network, which was the second means through which Mazzini sought to transform the perception of Italy and of Italians themselves. Through the careful cultivation of activists and sympathisers, he promoted the ideal of Italian 'resurrection' in literary and political circles outside Italy. By the 1840s Mazzini knew most of literary London, and these contacts gave him influence in the press and an unparalleled access to the expanding liberal public sphere in Britain and elsewhere.[46] Mazzini was also assiduous in encouraging personal friendships with liberal men and women for political purposes. He used his considerable personal magnetism and the romantic image of a lonely, suffering exile as a means of attracting 'disciples' to work for the Italian cause, and he met with considerable success, perhaps especially in recruiting women as supporters, fund-raisers and activists ('I have a Legion of Ladies who love me madly' he wrote to his mother in 1847).[47] He used his location in London as the basis for a Young Italy network in Europe and in North and South America, and he also established links to other political exiles in London and through them to radical groups elsewhere as well.[48]

The success of this second strategy is well documented. It helped to create a vast international network of associates, supporters and influential friends of Italian freedom on whose public and private support Mazzini was able to rely from the 1840s onwards. This network was subsequently to play a decisive role in the general shift of public opinion against Austria during the 1850s, and the money and press campaigns which it organised played a crucial role during the events of Italian unification in 1859–61.

It thus seems beyond doubt that Mazzini achieved practical political results through the press and through his network of supporters. However, this success may also seem to be in striking contrast with the results of Mazzini's third strategy, based on direct action through revolutionary conspiracies, violent insurrections and military expeditions, which so many historians and contemporaries, as we saw above, have judged as failures. Still I would suggest that there is another way of assessing these failed insurrections. If we see them not merely as efforts at rapid regime change but as displays of political protest and belonging, or as what Sudhir Hazareesingh has called exercises in 'political imagination', these events seem to have had a considerable impact.[49] They were part of a process whereby Mazzini sought to invent and communicate a new political culture in Italy, based around an idea of the nation and complete with its own rituals, narratives and symbols; and indeed, the experiences of protest, rebellion and (perhaps inevitable) repression helped shape the political consciousness of a generation and give them a sense of themselves as an alternative political elite.

For instance, Mazzini was harshly criticised when an 1844 expedition organised to 'liberate' Calabria by the Venetian brothers Attilio and Emilio Bandiera ended in catastrophe with their capture and execution. Yet Mazzini turned the disaster into a propaganda opportunity. Declaring that '[t]o foresee the future of a cause or of a people, I know no better method than to study the history of its Martyrs', he published an extended eulogy to the Bandiera brothers' heroism in the English radical weekly *The People's Journal*, recasting the story of their expedition as a tragic tale of decadence, rebellion, betrayal and redemption.[50] Mazzini's cultivation of London's liberal intellectuals also paid dividends at this time. When it emerged that his letters had been intercepted by the British government and passed on to the government in Vienna, a huge public and parliamentary outcry resulted which gave free publicity to Italian nationalism and to Mazzini in particular. Mazzini's friend, the liberal historian Thomas Carlyle, wrote a letter to *The Times* extolling Mazzini's 'genius and virtue' and his 'sterling veracity, humanity, and nobleness of mind'.[51] Mazzini became something of a popular hero, and pictures of him were sold all over

London. Moreover, as a result of his efforts, the Bandieras became the subject of a popular cult. They took their place in a patriotic canon as the first modern martyrs of the new Italy; and their journey, actions and ultimate sacrifice was established as an exemplary narrative which inspired both Pisacane's disastrous expedition to Sapri in 1857 and Garibaldi's triumphant conquest of Sicily in 1860.

This reappraisal of Mazzini's role in the Risorgimento allows us to answer at least some of the questions raised at the end of the first section of this chapter. Mazzini's fervent belief that the relationship between God and the people was fulfilled in the existence of nations, together with his conviction, inherited from the Jacobins, that political change held the key to transforming people's material and spiritual existence drove him and his followers to political agitation against all the odds. His great skill as a propagandist shifted the political terms of debate in the peninsula into the simple and enduring set of oppositions between nation and particularism, progress and reaction. As a proselytiser for the Italian nation he galvanised international public opinion behind the idea of Risorgimento. His insurrectionary methods often led to disaster, but they also attracted publicity, helped create a collective identity and could on occasion, if perhaps only fully effectively with Garibaldi in 1860, be spectacularly successful. It was Mazzini who successfully recast the instability of Restoration Italy as the unfulfilled demand of a nation to be free, and it was his movement which first harnessed the appeal of a cultural identity and successfully attached it to a revolutionary claim for legitimate political power.

1848 and beyond

The events of 1848–49 and their political consequences were discussed in chapter one. In the aftermath of 1848, there occurred a change in the fortunes both of the political opposition and the Restoration regimes. After the series of failed insurrections in the mid-1850s, which attracted bad publicity for the movement, Mazzinianism lost a great deal of a political ground and many previously loyal Mazzinians abandoned their leader. Meanwhile the moderate liberal movement led by D'Azeglio gained a foothold in Piedmont; under Cavour after 1852, it attracted an increasingly large following and achieved significant political and economic success.

The divisions between Mazzinians and moderate liberals persisted, however, and defined many aspects of the crisis of 1859–61, which led to the unification of Italy, as well as political life in united Italy thereafter. As we saw in chapter 3, the Restoration governments, with the exception of Piedmont, experienced a steadily increasing (and, in retrospect, evidently terminal) crisis of legitimacy, which their lurch to the right and towards policies of repression did little or nothing to resolve. Financially unstable, condemned internationally and, for the first time, genuinely unpopular, the Kingdom of the Two Sicilies, the Papal States and even the hitherto more reformist Grand Duchy of Tuscany lost the precarious balance between conservatism and modernisation which had characterised their regimes for intermittent periods during the 1830s and early 1840s.

This changing political environment was paralleled by changes in the nature and impact of nationalism. An enduring consequence of the 1848–49 revolutions was the development of a potent nationalist mythology around the events of these years. The popular uprising during the 'five days' of Milan (March 1848); the heroic defence of both the Roman and the Venetian Republics (summer 1849); and Garibaldi's retreat from Rome through the Apennines in an attempt to reach, and help defend, Venice were widely publicised in the national and international press and made heroes of Mazzini, Garibaldi and Daniele Manin (the head of the Venetian Republic). Thereafter, the moments, places and protagonists of the revolutions became part of nationalist memory, the subject of histories, memoirs, paintings and novels. With the creation of a new nationalist diaspora in the wake of defeat and political repression, the fame of 1848–49 (Italy's 'first war of Independence') and of Italian nationalist struggle spread far and wide: first to liberal Piedmont, which welcomed many exiles from the other Italian states, then to France, England and the United States.

It was in Piedmont that the strengthening of nationalism had the most dramatic consequences. The defeat of the 1848–49 revolutions with Austrian and French assistance added force to the nationalist argument that foreign domination was the root of modern Italy's political ills. As a result, more and more moderate liberals began to consider nationalism as a reasonable political ideology.

Before the 1840s, the moderate liberal interest in Italy was expressed in a great enthusiasm for Italian history and culture, and in a series of publishing and other cultural ventures, notably around the journals *Il Conciliatore* in Milan and *L'Antologia* in Florence.[52] However, its political articulation was confined to a generic, if sometimes strongly felt, anti-Austrianism. During the 1840s, a wave of nationalist literature and cultural activity spread across the towns of northern and central Italy, and a renewed enthusiasm for nationalist questions and interests were especially clear in publishing: from the founding of the periodical *Il Politecnico* by Carlo Cattaneo in Milan to the enthusiasm which created Massimo d'Azeglio's historical novel *Ettore Fieramosca*.[53]

It was at this point that many moderates became fervent supporters of what was called 'neo-Guelphism'. As we saw in chapter 1, this movement was the result of a proposal put forward by the Piedmontese priest Vincenzo Gioberti, in a hugely popular book *Il primato morale e civile degli Italiani* first published in 1843, for an Italian confederation with the Pope as President. Gioberti's fusion of Catholic universalism with a cultural and political idea of Italy had enormous appeal, largely because it appeared to reconcile Catholicism with moderate ideas of economic progress and political liberalism.[54] In 1846, the project was seemingly endorsed by the election of Pope Pius IX, an apparent liberal, and the support of the Piedmontese king, Carlo Alberto. And although the Pope's condemnation of the war on Austria in the spring of 1848, and his political actions thereafter, destroyed these hopes, a diffuse sense of political nationalism remained and conditioned moderate liberal politics throughout the 1850s. As a result of the political upheavals of the 1840s and thereafter, moderate liberals developed a nationalist programme which became a powerful ideological and political alternative to Mazzinianism.

After 1849, as the only Italian state not to re-impose press censorship and restrictions on public assembly, Piedmont became the centre of renewed nationalist activity. Encouraged by the arrival of political exiles from elsewhere in Italy, many of whom were writers, journalists and/or publishers seeking contacts and gainful employment in their new home, newspapers and periodicals of a nationalist character proliferated. From 1857, moreover, such press activity was given a political focus with the organisation of the Italian National Society by Daniele Manin, Giorgio Pallavicino Trivulzio and Giuseppe La Farina, all exiles since the events of 1848–49.

The campaigns of the National Society, and especially those of its newspaper *Il Piccolo Corriere d'Italia* (whose news items became dedicated entirely to promoting the issue of national unification within Piedmont and to persuading nationalists elsewhere of the necessity of endorsing Piedmontese leadership), played a vital role in making nationalism respectable among the educated middle classes of Italy. The Society's activities – the circulation of pamphlets, posters and printed images; the promotion and reporting of patriotic slogans and public demonstrations – contributed significantly to the wave of nationalist (and anti-Austrian) enthusiasm which swept the towns and cities of the Italian peninsula in the late 1850s. Through its publishing activities, the National Society played a crucial part in creating and maintaining a common nationalist outlook among its members and adherents, and in presenting 'a simple picture of Italy on the threshold of unity, preparing to fight beside Piedmont.'[55]

The use of the press to promote the idea of Italy as a political nation, and its widespread acceptance, shows how far Mazzinian ideas – dismissed as 'foolish' and 'useless' only a decade before – had penetrated political debate, even as Mazzinianism declined as a political movement. The National Society had practical consequences too. Its leaders, especially the Sicilian exile Giuseppe La Farina, helped to persuade Cavour that a useful alternative to revolutionary nationalism existed. Cavour, and other leading moderate liberals like Bettino Ricasoli and Marco Minghetti, came to see in the language of nationalism a means of emphasising their own political interests, and pitting them against those of conservative

Figure 6.1   'The Kiss' (*Il bacio*), Francesco Hayez, 1859.
Pinacoteca Brera, Milan, Italy.

In this famous painting by the leading Risorgimento artist Hayez, a soldier
bids his lover farewell in a passionate embrace. Despite its setting in the
fourteenth century, the image was instantly recognisable as an allusion to
the 1859 war against Austria and the young men who left their homes to
fight for Italy. This picture and the next reflect the great interest in and
enthusiasm for these military events.

Figure 6.2   Volunteers for the 1859 war against Austria.
C. Paya *Histoire de la guerre d'Italie*, Paris, 1860. © Bibliothèque nationale de France, Paris, France.

This is a contemporary illustration from a French publication on the war. The calmness of this scene was deliberate, as the governments of both Piedmont and France were anxious to stress the gentlemanly and respectable qualities of their military volunteers. Note, however, the presence of the 'people' in the two more roughly dressed figures and the reference to the popularity of the volunteer movement (a long queue of men forms out and beyond the door).

Austria. Specifically for Cavour, nationalism seemed to offer a significant opportunity for endorsing the economic development of northern Italy independently from Austria. At the same time, as the international climate turned against the conservatives when Austria and Russia fell out over the war in the Crimea (1853–56), and the French and British governments adopted a more favourable attitude towards Italian national sentiment, Cavour perceived an advantage in speaking on behalf of Italy, and about Italy's repression by Austria, in the international arena. The prestige that this defence of Italy gave to Piedmont made its king, Vittorio Emanuele II, another late convert to the nationalist cause.

In turn, Cavour's apparent approval of the idea of Italy gave nationalism greater respectability; it meant that nationalism became associated with political stability instead of revolutionary violence. The National Society was not slow to take advantage of this shift. By 1859, the National Society dominated liberal circles in central Italy, and during the war of 1859 it encouraged and oversaw the large-scale movement of military volunteers into Piedmont from Lombardy and central Italy. It was instrumental in winning support in central Italy for union with Piedmont, and was responsible for organising the plebiscites which voted for union with the same in the spring of 1860. Garibaldi's initial expedition to Sicily was made possible by money raised by the National Society, and by the guns donated to him by La Farina.

United Italy

The crisis of Mazzinianism after 1849, and its decline as a political force, needs to be reassessed. National unity, the primary objective of most Mazzinians after 1849 and for which they were prepared to sacrifice their republican ideals at this time, became something of a reality in 1859–61. Garibaldi's expedition to Sicily was in many ways a triumph of Mazzinian methods.

Garibaldi's overthrow of Bourbon government obliged Cavour to go far outside his original intention of expelling Austria from northern Italy. Instead, Cavour was forced to mastermind the unification of northern Italy with the southern Kingdom of the Two Sicilies, a part of Italy in which he had no interest. Hence, his 'nationalist' policies in 1859 and 1860 reflect his political ambitions for Piedmont, not Italy; they demonstrate the role of diplomacy and dynasty in the unification of the peninsula and were in many ways a cynical exercise in limiting the damage caused by Garibaldi. Yet Cavour's reaction to the events of 1860 reflects equally the capacity of Mazzinians to use propaganda and insurrection in order to wrongfoot their adversaries, so precipitating them into political action. Cavour's behaviour towards Garibaldi also shows the immense popularity of the latter, a popularity which was the fruit of a long and successful publicity campaign structured and organised initially by Mazzini.

Cavour's actions in 1859-60 were cynical and elitist, but they point just as much to the legitimacy which the idea of Italian unification had acquired in public opinion and politics. As historians, we should of course remember what previous research has shown us about the aims of Cavour; we can also question the logic of national unification in 1860 and recognise its 'accidental character'. Still, we must also accept the findings of the new cultural history and acknowledge the outwardly unstoppable appeal of nationalism as a large-scale movement: to most (if, of course, not all) educated contemporaries, national unification seemed the most viable and attractive solution to the political crisis prevailing in Italy at this time.

Yet the events of 1860 also mark a profound defeat for Mazzini and Garibaldi at the hands of Cavour, just as the organisation of the National Society signals an important transformation in the aims and methods of the Italian nationalist movement. Moderate liberals and republicans may have shared the same cultural idea of Italy, and they spoke the same political language derived from this culture, but the political meanings which they attached to terms like 'nation', 'liberty' and 'resurrection' were quite distinct. The shift from revolutionary conspiracy and popular insurrection towards the respectability of parliamentary debate and diplomacy could not but alter the political nature of nationalism itself. Specifically, by allying itself to Piedmont, the National Society endorsed a conservative and monarchical political tradition, while the link between its leaders and Cavour involved their implicit acceptance of, and subordination to, his essentially material ambitions. The National Society relegated revolution to a secondary phase, and deprived nationalism of its moral, regenerative force. As Raymond Grew, historian of the National Society, comments: '[t]he concept of the Risorgimento was being changed from a revolution that would remake society to a merely political change brought about by the force of arms'.[56]

So, united Italy was the creation of kings not of the people. It left (albeit temporarily as it turned out) Rome and Venice outside its borders, and in the hands of the Pope and the Austrians – the designated enemies of Italian nationality. Thanks to nationalist propaganda efforts over the preceding three decades, Cavour's unification of the peninsula in 1860 may have seemed the solution to Italy's political crisis but, as we have seen in the chapters in this book on government, society and the economy, the reality was far more complicated. Unification also created new problems of its own. Most notably, it was achieved at the cost of an irreparable and damaging rift with the Church in Italy, and it destroyed for ever the hope of reconciling the Pope to Italian nationalism. It is in this awkward passage from cultural to political nationalism, and in nationalism's equally troubled transition from revolutionary to official ideology, that the sources for so much of the controversy surrounding Italian unification can be found.

7

Italian Unification

Liberal Italy

After 1860, the 'poetry' of the Risorgimento gave way to the 'prose' of the post-Risorgimento. The creation of the Kingdom of Italy was a disappointment in many ways. The failure immediately to include Venetia and Rome within the new state seemed a striking admission of national weakness. Rome was an especially potent symbol of Italian unity and strength, and its absence from liberal Italy was felt very acutely. Rome only became part of the Italian Kingdom in 1870, when defeat in the Franco-Prussian war obliged Napoleon III to withdraw the French garrison from Rome, but at the price of a permanent breach between Church and state. Pope Pius IX henceforth withdrew as a self-proclaimed 'prisoner' into the Vatican, and a papal encyclical of 1874 (*Non expedit*) threatened Catholics with excommunication if they participated in Italian politics. Venetia was won from the Austrians earlier, in 1866, but only after a humiliating defeat by the Austrian navy and army had served to emphasise Italy's lack of independence and military power. Other Italian regions, most notably the Trentino and the port of Trieste, remained part of the Austrian Empire ('unredeemed' in nationalist parlance) until after the First World War.

Italy experienced other immediate difficulties in the first few decades of national government. Popular unrest did not cease with the collapse of the Restoration states. The explosion of rural banditry in the South and Sicily, and urban riots in Turin and Milan, created severe public-order crises throughout the 1860s. During the war against Austria in 1866, anti-government rebels

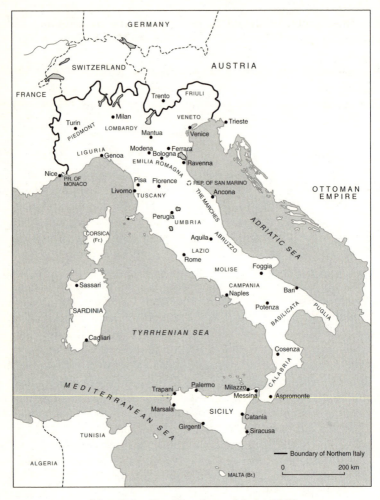

Map 7.1 The Kingdom of Italy, 1870

occupied the city of Palermo and held it for a week in defiance of government authority. During the 1870s, parts of central and southern Italy became major strongholds of anarchist activity.

These problems should be seen against the background of a financial crisis and slow economic growth. The growing budget deficit, a legacy of Cavour's pursuit of economic growth in the 1850s and the wars of 1859–60, led to a convertibility crisis in 1866 and to the decision in 1868 to reinstate the *macinato* (grist) tax, an unpopular tax associated with the old regime. The expected benefits of free trade were slow to materialise too. They brought prosperity to areas of commercial agriculture, but dealt a sometimes devastating blow to manufacturing industry, particularly in the South.

Political life in the new Italy was also a source of dissatisfaction. In reality, the success of liberal Piedmont during the 1850s had always masked a much more unstable reality. Cavour's hold on power was shaky, the scale of his commitment to liberalism and reform could be questioned, and his aggressive foreign and religious policies won him as many enemies as friends. After unification, Cavour's decision (emphasised by his successors) to 'piedmontise' all existing administrative institutions and impose a centralised political structure on the rest of Italy, was unpopular in all of the former states. It served to emphasise rather than undermine regional rivalries and local resistance. Furthermore, centralisation was accompanied by a parliamentary system based on a narrow suffrage (2 per cent of the population) and by a repressive policy towards popular unrest that seemed to be little different from the practices of the old regime. Then Cavour's sudden death in June 1861 left the new Italy without any obvious leader, and added to the general atmosphere of political instability.

Underlying all these problems was the more long-term failure of the unified state to embody national unity, to establish political consensus or to join the apparently wealthy, urban North to an impoverished, rural South. Members of the Left opposition in the Italian parliament (former Mazzinians, radicals and federalists) emphasised these problems for political purposes; they challenged and subverted official attempts to glorify the Risorgimento and argued instead that Italy's 'resurrection' had been betrayed, defeated and diverted. But they were not alone. Reflecting on the problems of the South, Massimo d'Azeglio, an opponent of Mazzini and one of the founders of moderate liberalism, wrote: 'there must have been some mistake somewhere. Our principles and our policy must be wrong'. 'Whose fault is it?', asked Pasquale Villari, professor of history and politician of the Right, after the disastrous war of 1866, and he offered his own answer. Italy had at home 'an enemy which is stronger than Austria:

> I refer to our colossal ignorance, our multitudes of illiterates, our machine bureaucrats, childish politicians, ignoramus professors, hopeless diplomats, incapable generals, unskilled workers, primitive farmers, and the rhetoric which gnaws our very bones.[1]

As we have seen, many of these sentiments were echoed in the work of later historians. Perhaps most fully in Marxist analyses, the shortcomings of liberal Italy were explained by reference to the failures of national unification and the Risorgimento. The 'passive' nature of Italy's revolution had led, it was argued, to a weak middle-class leadership and, hence, to the reliance on coercion rather than popular consent as a basis for government. The economic 'backwardness' of liberal Italy was also attributed to this passive revolution and, specifically, to the failure to eradicate feudalism and allow capitalism to develop. One great attraction of this approach was how much it explained. It suggested that Italy's economic and political development in the nineteenth century had a single, discernible pattern. The experiences of liberal Italy, its failure to develop as a full parliamentary democracy and, as a result, its eventual collapse into fascism, could all be traced back to the process of national unification and to the struggles of the Risorgimento.

Historical understandings of the Risorgimento are thus difficult to separate from the circumstances of Italian unification and its troubled aftermath. Most noticeably, the perception of failure and decline, which drove much of Risorgimento rhetoric, persisted and was consolidated thereafter. What Silvana Patriarca calls the discourse on Italian virtues and vices, or the sense that just as there was something noble about Italy so there was something weak about the national character, became an entrenched and unquestioned part of public debate. Looking into the Italian past in order to explain the failings of the present drove the historical as well as the political agenda.[2]

State formation

During the 1980s and 1990s, the work of revisionist historians comprehensively challenged these discourses of virtues, vices and failure; and historians also went to work to dissolve the connections between economic, social and political change which were the mainstay of older historical approaches to the Risorgimento. Taken together with similar research on the experiences of other European nations like Britain, Germany and France, this process of revision allows us both to deny that Italy was ever that 'peculiar' and to outline a new explanation for its specific path to the modern world.

Italy's particular experiences as a nation can be partly attributed to problems of modern state formation, and here comparison is extremely helpful. In all the major European countries including Italy, the Restoration period was marked by economic crises, social unrest, the growth of political opposition and disagreements between and among the ruling elites. In this respect, there was nothing unusual about Italy. Still, a number of other factors do distinguish the Italian experience from the British, French or German cases in this period, namely, Italy's weak international position, the difficulty of maintaining its territorial integrity, and the problem of the Church. In addition, the general failure of internal reform in the years before 1860 (Piedmont is an exception) made it extremely difficult for the Restoration states (other than Piedmont) to withstand the massive political crisis of 1859–61. Moreover, none of these problems were solved by unification.

The greater vulnerability of the Restoration states to international pressure was a major factor in their decline and fall. Between 1815 and 1860, Italy's political destiny was to a considerable extent decided by statesmen in Vienna, Paris and London, and Austrian protection after 1815 meant that the fortunes of Italy's Restoration states rose and fell with Austria. Thus, until the defeat of Austria in

1859, the Restoration states could for the most part ignore internal pressure for political change. With the defeat of Austria, this pressure rapidly became overwhelming. In turn, Italy's lack of independence in the international arena conditioned the outcome of 1859–60, and here the rise of Prussia and Bismarck's creation of a new super-power in Europe ten years later forms a striking contrast to Piedmont's more compromised championing of the 'Italian Question'. After 1860, foreign policy considerations, and specifically the necessity of demonstrating the integrity and viability of the new state to the European powers, influenced the decision to unify Italy's administrative structures rapidly and to repress popular and political unrest.[3]

The problem of maintaining territorial integrity seems to have been more acute in Italy than elsewhere. Generally speaking, the experience of state formation in nineteenth-century Europe was easier, and far more peaceful, in smaller, more compact states such as those of South-West Germany, or in those with a longer, consolidated history of territorial unity.[4] In Italy, local, elite-led resistance to administrative modernisation and centralisation challenged the integrity of many Restoration states. Most notably in the Two Sicilies and the Papal States, but also in Piedmont-Liguria and Venetia, this resistance threatened the process of reform. So the risk of internal collapse also contributed to the crisis of Restoration government. And in view of the outcome of the events of 1859–60, it is not surprising that after 1860 the same problem of maintaining territorial control in a now far larger political entity, with no history of administrative unity, persisted and grew worse. Local and regional resistance to the new central power after 1860 continued to frustrate the process of bureaucratic modernisation, and undermined efforts to construct a sense of national identity.[5]

The hostile attitude of the Church to a united Italy further weakened both the state's legitimacy and its infrastructural power. The Church's attitude and the physical presence of the Pope in Italy perhaps account for the real distinctiveness of the Italian experience. Although the struggle between Church and state was a prominent feature of nation-state formation in France and Germany, only in Italy was the Church's temporal power under threat. In this respect, and in striking contrast to political nationalism in Ireland

and in parts of Eastern Europe (arguably the nations most similar to, and affected by, the Italian case), Italian nationalism after 1848 was set on a direct collision course with the Catholic Church. The collision, which came about with national unification, emphasised the 'national' power of the Church and the fragility of the secular 'Italian' state.

When Pope Pius IX obliged Italians to choose between their loyalty to the Church and their support of the new state, he dealt

Figure 7.1 The forward march of the nation.

G. Oddo, *I mille di Marsala. Scene Rivoluzionarie*, Milan, 1863. Società Siciliana per la Storia Patria, Palermo, Italy.

This print from 1863 shows Garibaldi, the King Vittorio Emanuele II (on the left) and 'Italy' (in the centre) trampling over a Jesuit priest (the symbol of Papal oppression) in their common drive to unite the nation. Though effective as a piece of political rhetoric, this print ignores the underlying disunity in liberal Italy and the continuing strength and popularity of the Church.

a devastating blow to the legitimacy of liberal Italy. Pius IX, unlike the new state, possessed both the moral and the institutional power to enforce his instructions. The beliefs, rituals and language of the Catholic Church united Italians, as Gioberti had noted in the 1840s, in ways that a sense of secular nationhood did not. In the overwhelming majority of cases, the Church's control of education and charity also gave priests a hold over local politics that the liberal state, for all its claim to represent a new bureaucratic authority, could never aspire to.

Building the nation

In the course of the preceding chapters we have seen that, during the Risorgimento, the logic of political modernisation, as well as economic and social change, tended if anything towards a further fracturing of the peninsula rather than to greater unity or uniformity. Administrative centralisation was not a success, and, economically and socially, Italy was probably becoming less rather than more 'national'. There is also little to suggest that the creation of a single, unitary state was the solution to the crisis of Restoration Italy. It is in this way that nationalism and the drive to national unity can be seen as part of Italy's problem: as we noted in chapter 5, unification can even be called an economic mistake, the result of political over-ambition and Great Power diplomacy.

Yet, somewhat perversely, the weakness of Italian nationalism as a political solution points to its strength as a mobilising ideology. Many of Cavour's actions between 1859 and 1861, especially his courting of Garibaldi and the National Society and the invasion of the Papal States, identify less tangible factors determining government policy. National unification tells us that liberal leaders in Piedmont and elsewhere were not only affected by the material arguments of modernisation, but that they were also conditioned by the emotional appeal of unitary nationalism. At the least, we can say that they found it impossible to ignore the political impact of nationalism's powerful rhetoric and popularity, however unrealistic the aims of nationalists may have been.

The strange mix of strength and weakness characteristic of

Italian nationalism in the Risorgimento can also be observed in the post-Risorgimento. Many of the policies pursued by the leaders of liberal Italy reflected an acute awareness both of the importance of nationalism and of the problems which it caused. The need to 'make Italians' drove investment in infrastructure, the expansion of the army, and reforms in education in the 1860s and 1870s. Especially after the parliamentary Left came to power in 1876, these efforts were increased and expanded into new areas of cultural life. The symbols, rites and festivals of Roman Catholicism were appropriated in an effort to create a new 'civic religion', and the Risorgimento was rewritten as a foundation story and 'place of memory', intended to give Italians the sense of a common past.

After his death in 1878, King Vittorio Emanuele II's body was buried in the Pantheon in Rome, and in 1884 there was a mass, national pilgrimage to his tomb. Commemorative events such as Constitution Day (*la festa dello Statuto*), established in Piedmont in 1851, continued after unification, and newer festivals, such as the huge choreographed parade of 20 September (celebrating the breach of Rome's Porta Pia and the taking of Rome in 1870) inaugurated in 1895, were organised. During the 1880s and after, museums of the Risorgimento were opened throughout Italy. New public spaces and monuments – most famously the Victor Emmanuel monument (*Vittoriano*) in Rome – were created to celebrate the Risorgimento.[6]

Yet with all this, the prevailing sense is that nationalism failed to unite Italians: that the whole idea was 'flawed and problematic in the first place' and that the mass of the people remained 'alienated and indifferent'.[7] There is now a substantial historical literature dedicated to the process of nation-building in liberal Italy. Much of it is driven by the assumption that nation-building simply reflected the feebleness of national identity, and there is an equally general consensus that all these efforts to make Italians fell short of their desired results and did little to create or cement strong feelings of national belonging.

Once again, however, the pervasive sense of failure associated with Italian nationalism obscures a more subtle reality. First, research outside Italy suggests that there was nothing unusual about the Italian case, and that similar state-sponsored policies of nationalisation met with popular resistance across Europe. In any

Figure 7.2 Victor Emmanuel monument (*Vittoriano*) in Rome.

Constructed in the centre of Rome next to the Capitoline hill, this monument to the first King of Italy is one of the most dramatic expressions of the drive to 'make Italians' after national unification. Like nation-building itself, however, the monument was very controversial. It took decades to build and destroyed half of the Capitoline Hill (along with its priceless archaeological evidence) in the process. The monument's garish appearance also made it unpopular with Romans who invented a number of derisive names for it: 'the wedding cake', 'the typewriter' and '*zuppa inglese*' ('trifle').

case, popular participation was probably never the primary concern of these festivities; they aimed more at the 'representation of a political and social body accompanied by codified demonstrations of a popular presence.'[8] In other words, these events were never meant to be popular: their purpose instead was to act out official rituals from which the public was largely excluded. Moreover, while there is little doubt that as a uniform and official ideology there were problems with 'making Italians', there is also evidence to suggest that it was far more effective as a partisan ideology, or as an ideology of political and religious resistance. In this sense, the sense of failure associated with official nation-building after unification points to the persistence of a successful and potent nationalist rhetoric which, much as it had done under the Restoration, provided the basis for political opposition. Italian nationalism flourished after unification, but it opposed the Italian people to its apparently inadequate rulers.[9]

At the same time, the focus on the failure of festivals and monuments may hide other areas of political life which assumed the character of a civic religion. Theatre, music and literature continued to reflect a nationalist sensibility, and the King and the royal family steadily acquired a national role and significance. There was what Catherine Brice has called 'an infinity of other forms of "participation"': a proliferation of patriotic publications and other ephemera, such as letters, illustrated pamphlets, poems, pictures and other souvenirs dedicated to famous moments in, and personalities of, the Risorgimento. It can be argued that an effective civic religion was established in liberal Italy after 1861, but it was expressed in quite traditional forms, and based on interpersonal relations and feelings of deference.[10] So, for the purposes of understanding nation-building in Italy, the older historiographical paradigm which associated the Risorgimento and nationalism with 'progress' again seems insufficient; recent research has revealed the process to have been a very varied mixture of tradition and modernity in which a modern sense of belonging to the nation was intertwined with more customary forms and expressions of identity.

Nation-building may have been more successful than we suppose, or have made its impact in different ways or different places. It seems clear, for example, that after unification there was an almost seamless transfer of the language and themes of the nationalist discourse into political debate, and Alberto Banti has written that in liberal Italy 'there is not a speech made by a political leader ... in which there are not recurring references to "Italy", "fatherland", "nation", and "people', using them as key words to identify the community to which one belongs and which one is addressing.'[11] After 1870, the 'culture wars' between Church and state were also dominated by patriotic language and images which melded seamlessly with the religious.

The Risorgimento and the Italian nation

Nationalism is an ideology built on eclecticism, which appeals to a traditional sense of community by harnessing modern communication techniques and by borrowing and manipulating bits of new and existing discourse and practice. A study of Italian national identity shows us that this process can be immensely seductive and successful but that there are limits to how far it can be taken and what it can achieve. In this regard, there are number of questions about Italian nationalism which remain unanswered or unexplored. To go back to Banti's comments: we still know comparatively little about the popular reception of Italian nationalist 'references'; we don't know whether, if ever or how key words such as 'Italy' or 'fatherland' were accepted by a broader section of the population or if they were used by those – such as Catholics – who rejected the legitimacy of liberal Italy.

Nationalist key words may have endured over time, but did they mean the same thing? We should not assume that they did: a continuity of discourse is not equivalent to a continuity in political ideas and action. As I pointed out in the previous chapter, moderate liberals and democrats used the same language in the Risorgimento but they attached different political meanings to it. Similarly, if we turn to fascism, key words like 'nation' and 'people' had quite distinct political articulations for liberals, on the one hand, and for fascists, on the other. And in order to arrive at a more complete understanding of the nationalist discourse and its impact, both in the long nineteenth and in the shorter twentieth centuries, we need also to analyse how nationalist language and symbols were variously appropriated or rejected by the socialist, right and/or clerical movements in the decades between Italian unification and the First World War. We might also want to examine how the political meanings of these same nationalist key words shifted during fascism, after its collapse and even in early post-war Italy.[12]

But let us return to the Risorgimento. Many other questions remain about the connections and discontinuities between Risorgimento culture and the political culture of liberal Italy. For instance: to what extent did national unification – the move from nationalism as an opposition movement to nationalism as the offi-

cial ideology of a regime – represent a break with the political rhetoric and practices created during the struggles of the Risorgimento?
Did the relationship between public and private change with unification; and how did patriotic women respond to the new political
situation and how were they affected?[13] In what ways did the overlapping networks of friendship, family and politics, which had
sustained Risorgimento patriots before 1861, persist into the political structures of liberal Italy? Specifically, how did these personal
networks affect the conduct of public life and the formation of political parties? More complete answers to these questions should help
us better to understand the intricate relationship between nationalism, Risorgimento, political unification, and its long aftermath.

Yet, in the end, the link between the Risorgimento and national
unification may prove difficult to break. No other European nation
had a 'Risorgimento' and none described these experiences in such
conspicuously romantic terms. Over a century and a half of political, social and cultural change separates the present-day reader
from the Risorgimento patriots, and prevents us in many ways
from penetrating their world. Their ideas of Italy, of fatherland,
people and revolution, may seem absurd (or worse) to us, but it is
precisely this gulf of practice and understanding that we should
seek to analyse and understand. Even clichés have content: the
myths and stereotypes of nationalism are also a form of historical
evidence.[14] In order to deconstruct national myths, we cannot
simply dismiss or decry them but we should seek instead to understand their structure, meaning, appeal and impact.

If we want to explain why the process of change unleashed by
the French Revolution and the Restoration resulted in Italian unification, it is vital to analyse and take account of the political and
emotional appeal of nationalism. The 'poetry' of the Risorgimento,
and its potency as a foundation story for the new Italy, may have
blinded nationalists to the equally powerful divisions within
Italian society, but their drive for national unity and/or independence drastically altered the outcome of all the other trends – state
formation, economic development and social conflict – which
affected the Italian peninsula at this time. The poetry of the
Risorgimento may not explain the prose of the post-Risorgimento,
and it does not account for the complex process of modernisation

Notes

2 The Risorgimento and the History of Italy

1. *Ultime lettere di Jacopo Ortis* (1798) and *Dei sepolcri* (1807), quoted in C. Duggan, *The Force of Destiny. A History of Italy since 1796* (London, 2007), pp. 3, 35.
2. S. Berger, M. Donovan and K. Passmore (eds), *Writing National Histories. Western Europe since 1800* (London, 1999).
3. D. Mack Smith (ed.), *The Making of Italy, 1796–1866* (London, 1968), pp. 363–4.
4. Duggan, *The Force of Destiny*, pp. 90–101; D. Laven, 'Italy the Idea of the Nation in the Risorgimento and Liberal Eras', in T. Baycroft and M. Hewitson (eds), *What is a Nation? Europe 1789–1914* (Oxford, 2006), pp. 268–9; A. Lyttelton, 'Creating a National Past: History, Myth and Image in the Risorgimento', in A. R. Ascoli and K. von Henneberg, *Making and Remaking Italy. The Cultivation of National Identity around the Risorgimento* (Oxford, 2001), pp. 27–74.
5. R. Dainotto, '"Tramonto" and "Risorgimento": Gentile's Dialectics and the Prophecy of Nationhood', in Ascoli and von Henneberg, *Making and Remaking Italy*, pp. 241–55.
6. B. Croce, *A History of Italy, 1871–1915* (Oxford, 1929); A. Gramsci, *Il Risorgimento* (Turin, 1949), extracts published in Q. Hoare and G. Nowell Smith, *Selections from the Prison Notebooks of Antonio Gramsci* (London, 1971).
7. Croce, *A History of Italy*, p. 4.
8. R. Romeo, *Dal Piemonte sabaudo all'Italia liberale* (Turin, 1963), p. 128.
9. G. M. Trevelyan, *Garibaldi's Defence of the Roman Republic* (London, 1907); *Garibaldi and the Thousand* (London, 1909); *Garibaldi and the Making of Italy* (London, 1911).
10. D. Mack Smith, *Cavour and Garibaldi, 1860. A Study in Political Conflict* (Cambridge, 1985 [1954]).
11. A. J. P. Taylor, 'Cavour and Garibaldi', in *From Napoleon to the Second International* (London, 1995), pp. 265, 272.
12. P. Macry, *Ottocento. Famiglia, élites e patrimoni a Napoli* (Naples, 1988), pp. ix–x.
13. F. Rizzi, *La coccarda e le campane. Comunità rurali e repubblica romana nel Lazio (1848–1849)* (Milan, 1989), p. 230.
14. A. M. Banti, *Terra e denaro. Una borghesia padana dell'Ottocento* (Venice, 1989).

15. D. Laven, *Venice and Venetia under the Habsburgs, 1815–1835* (Oxford, 2002); M. Meriggi, *Il regno Lombardo-Veneto* (Turin, 1987) and *Amministrazione e classi sociali nel Lombardo-Veneto, 1814–1848* (Bologna, 1983).

16. N. Nada, *Dallo stato assoluto allo stato costituzionale. Storia del regno di Carlo Alberto dal 1831 al 1848* (Turin, 1980).

17. Among the key works are: M. Daunton, '"Gentlemanly Capitalism" and British Industry 1820–1914', *Past and Present*, 122 (1989), pp. 119–58; D. Blackbourn and G. Eley, *The Peculiarities of German History* (Oxford, 1984); F. Furet, *Interpreting the French Revolution* (Cambridge, 1981); A. J. Mayer, *The Persistence of the Old Regime. Europe to the Great War* (London, 1981).

18. A. M. Banti, *La nazione del Risorgimento. Parentela, santità e onore alle origini dell'Italia unita* (Turin, 2000); and for an indication of the direction of new research: A. M. Banti and P. Ginsborg (eds), *Storia d'Italia. Annali 22. Il Risorgimento* (Turin, 2007).

19. See the essays by Fernando Mazzocca, Simonetta Chiappini and Carlotta Sorba in Banti and Ginsborg (eds), *Storia d'Italia*. See also R. J. M. Olson, 'In the Dawn of Italy', in Olson (ed.), *Ottocento. Romanticism and Revolution in Nineteenth-Century Italian Painting* (New York, 1992). The starting point for research on cultural production is M. Berengo, *Intellettuali e librai nella Milano della Restaurazione* (Turin, 1980), but see also G. Albergoni, *I mestieri delle lettere tra istituzioni e mercato. Vivere e scrivere a Milano nella prima metà dell'Ottocento* (Milan, 2006).

20. See M. Isabella, *Risorgimento in Exile* (Oxford, forthcoming 2009).

21. See the essays by Roberto Bizzocchi, Ilaria Porciani, Marta Bonsanti, Luisa Levi d'Ancona, Simonetta Soldani, Laura Guidi, and Lucy Riall in Banti and Ginsborg (eds), *Storia d'Italia*.

22. L. Riall, *Garibaldi. Invention of a Hero* (New Haven and London, 2007); and see the essays by Alberto Banti and Pietro Finelli in Banti and Ginsborg (eds), *Storia d'Italia*.

3 The Politics of Restoration

1. A. O. Hirschmann, *The Rhetoric of Reaction* (Cambridge MA, 1991), pp. 8–10.

2. E. J. Hobsbawm, *The Age of Revolution, 1789–1848* (London, 1962), p. 138.

3. G. Candeloro, *Storia dell'Italia moderna, vol 2. Dalla restaurazione alla rivoluzione nazionale* (Milan, 1958), p. 23.

4. M. Berengo, 'Le origini del Lombardo-Veneto', *Rivista Storica Italiana*, 83 (1971), p. 544.

5. A. Aquarone, 'La politica legislativa della restaurazione nel regno di Sardegna', *Bolletino Storico Bibliografico Subalpino*, 57 (1959), pp. 21–50, 322–59.

6. M. Caravale and A. Caracciolo, *Lo stato pontificio da Martino V a Pio X* (Turin, 1978), pp. 606–12.
7. A. J. Reinerman, *Austria and the Papacy in the Age of Metternich,* vol. 2, *Revolution and Reaction 1830–1838* (Washington DC, 1989), pp. 35–80.
8. F. J. Coppa, *Cardinal Giacomo Antonelli and Papal Politics in European Affairs* (Albany NY, 1990), p. 45.
9. N. Nada, *Dallo stato assoluto alto stato costituzionale. Storia del regno di Carlo Alberto dal 1831 al 1848* (Turin, 1980).
10. M. Meriggi, *Amministrazione e classi sociale nel Lombardo-Veneto 1814–1848,* (Bologna, 1983), pp. 201–47. David Laven's research suggests that even this kind of opposition to the Austrian administration (at least in Venetia) has been overestimated: *Venice and Venetia under the Habsburgs, 1815–1835* (Cambridge, 2002), pp. 82–9.
11. P. Pezzino, 'Monarchia amministrativa ed *élites* locali: Naro nella prima metà dell'Ottocento', in P. Pezzino, *Un paradiso abitato dai diavoli. Società, élites, istituzioni nel Mezzogiorno contemporaneo* (Milan, 1992), pp. 159–76.
12. D. Laven, 'The Age of Restoration', in J. A. Davis (ed.), *Italy in the Nineteenth Century* (Oxford, 2000), p. 53.
13. L. Riall, 'Elites in Search of Authority. Political Power and Social Order in Nineteenth-Century Sicily', *History Workshop Journal,* 55 (2003), pp. 29–37; J. A. Davis, 'The Napoleonic Era in Southern Italy: An Ambiguous legacy?', *Proceedings of the British Academy,* 80 (1993), p. 148.
14. Laven, *Venice and Venetia,* p. 192.
15. C. Duggan, *The Force of Destiny. A History of Italy since 1796* (Oxford, 2007), p. 79.
16. A. J. Reinerman, 'The Failure of Popular Counter-Revolution in Risorgimento Italy: The Case of the Centurions, 1831–1847', *The Historical Journal,* 34 (1991), pp. 21–41.
17. J. A. Davis, *Naples and Napoleon. Southern Italy and the European Revolutions, 1780–1860* (Oxford, 2006), pp. 313–16; Meriggi, *Amministrazione e classi sociale*; Caravale and Caracciolo, *Lo stato pontificio.*
18. Of course, we should also look at the role of nationalism, and we can question the scale and stability of Cavour's achievement. These issues are discussed in chapters 6 and 7.

4 Social Conflict and Social Change

1. L. Cafagna, 'Se il risorgimento italiano sia stato una "rivoluzione borghese"', in L. Cafagna, *Dualismo e sviluppo nella storia d'Italia* (Venice, 1989), p. 161.
2. G. Prato, *Fatti e doctrine economiche alla vigilia del '48. L'Associazione Agraria Subalpina e il conte di Cavour* (Turin, 1920).

3. K. R. Greenfield, *Economics and Liberalism in the Risorgimento. A Study of Nationalism in Lombardy, 1814–1848* (Baltimore, MD, 1934).

4. *Selections from the Prison Notebooks of Antonio Gramsci,* edited and translated by Q. Hoare and G. Nowell Smith (London, 1971), p. 53.

5. Ibid., p. 79.

6. E. J. Hobsbawm, *The Age of Capital, 1848–1875* (London, 1975), p. 287.

7. A. J. Mayer, *The Persistence of the Old Regime. Europe to the Great War* (London, 1981), pp. 129–87.

8. G. Eley, 'Liberalism, Europe and the Bourgeoisie 1860–1914', in D. Blackbourn and R. J. Evans (eds), *The German Bourgeoisie* (London, 1991), pp. 293–317.

9. A. Lyttleton, 'The Middle Classes in Liberal Italy', in J. A. Davis and P. Ginsborg (eds), *Society and Politics in the Age of the Risorgimento* (Cambridge, 1991), p. 218.

10. M. Meriggi, 'La borghesia italiana', in J. Kocka (ed.), *Borghesie europee dell'Ottocento* (Venice, 1989), pp. 165–6,175.

11. L. Riall, 'Elites in Search of Authority. Political Power and Social Order in Nineteenth-Century Sicily', *History Workshop Journal*, 55 (2003), pp. 25–46; S. Lupo, 'Tra centro e periferia. Sui modi dell'aggregazione politica nel Mezzogiorno contemporaneo', in *Meridiana* 2 (1988), pp. 16–22.

12. A. M. Banti, *Terra e denaro. Una borghesia padana dell'ottocento* (Venice, 1989); M. Malatesta, *I signori della terra. L'organizzazione degli interessi agrari padani (1860–1914)* (Milan, 1989).

13. P. Ginsborg, *Daniele Manin and the Venetian Revolution of 1848–49* (Cambridge, 1979), p. 15.

14. T. Kroll, *La rivolta del patriziato. Il liberalismo della nobilità nella Toscana del Risorgimento* (Florence, 2005), pp. 83–111.

15. A. Cardoza, 'Tra caste e classe: clubs maschile dell'élite torinese, 1840–1914', *Quaderni Storici, 77* (1991), pp. 364–6.

16. A. M. Banti and M. Meriggi, 'Elites e associazioni nell'Italia dell'Ottocento: premessa', *Quaderni Storici, 77* (1991), p. 358.

17. D. L. Caglioti, *Associazionismo e sociabilità d'elite a Napoli nel xix secolo* (Naples, 1996); and on the theatre, see J. A. Davis, 'Opera and Absolutism in Restoration Italy, 1815–1860', *Journal of Interdisciplinary History*, xxxvi: 4 (2006), pp. 569–94.

18. Kroll, *La rivolta del patriziato*, pp. 113–216.

19. Quoted in O. Cancila, 'Palermo', in *Le città capitale degli stati pre-unitari. Atti del LIII Congresso del Istituto per la Storia del Risorgimento Italiano. 1986* (Rome, 1988), pp. 288, 291.

20. P. Macry, *Ottocento. Famiglia, élites e patrimoni a Napoli* (Turin, 1988), pp. xiii–xv, 259–62.

21. There is an important new literature on the relations between public and private in the Risorgimento, see especially: M. Bonsanti, 'Amore familiare, amore romantico e amor di patria' and L. Guidi, 'Donne e uomini del Sud sulle vie dell'esilio, 1848–60', both in A. M. Banti and

P. Ginsborg (eds), *Storia d'Italia, annali 22. Il Risorgimento* (Turin, 2007), pp. 127–52, 225–52; A. Russo, 'Tra fratello e sorella: Giuseppe ed Elisabetta Ricciardi. Linguaggi, strategie, idee politiche e religiose a confronto'and E. Sodini, 'Il buon nome della famiglia e l'amore per la patria: Felicita Bevilacqua e la lotteria patriottica', both in I. Porciani (ed.), *Famiglia e nazione nel lungo Ottocento italiano. Modelli, strategie, reti di relazioni* (Rome, 2006), pp. 83–105, 107–29.

22. E. di Ciommo, 'Elites provinciali e potere borbonico: note per una ricerca comparata', in A. Massafra (ed.), *Il Mezzogiorno preunitario. Economia, società e istituzioni* (Bari, 1988), pp. 967–8.

23. G. Fiume, 'Bandits, Violence and the Organisation of Power in Sicily in the Early Nineteenth Century', in Davis and Ginsborg (eds), *Society and Politics in the Age of the Risorgimento*, p. 84.

24. Riall, 'Elites in Search of Authority'; P. Pezzino, 'Introduzione: la modernizzazione violenta', in *Una certa reciprocità di favori. Mafia e modernizzazione violenta nella Sicilia postunitaria* (Milan, 1990).

25. Greenfield, *Economics and Liberalism in the Risorgimento*, pp. 30–1; Ginsborg, *Daniele Manin and the Venetian Revolution*, p. 23.

26. P. Brunello, *Ribelli, questuanti e banditi. Proteste contadine in Veneto e in Friuli, 1814–1866* (Venice, 1981), pp. 15–17, 102–4.

27. A. de Clementi, *Vivere nel latifondo. Le comunità della campagna laziale fra '700 e '800* (Milan, 1989); M. Caffiero, 'Usi e abusi: comunità rurali e difesa dell'economia tradizionale nello stato pontificio', *Passato e Presente*, 24 (1990), pp. 73–93.

28. J. A. Davis, 'Economy, Society and the State' in A. Davis (ed.), *Italy in the Nineteenth Century* (Oxford, 2000), p. 238.

29. L. Riall, '"Ill-contrived, badly executed [and] . . . of no avail"? Reform and its impact in the Sicilian *latifondo* (c.1770–c.1910)', in R. Halpern and E. dal Lago (eds), *The American South and the Italian Mezzogiorno: Essays in Comparative History* (London, 2002), pp. 132–53.

30. F. Rizzi, *La coccarde e le campane. Comunità rurali e repubblica romana nel Lazio (1848–1849)* (Milan, 1989).

31. L. Riall, *Garibaldi. Invention of a Hero* (New Haven and London, 2007), pp. 213–15, 273–85.

32. Brunello, *Ribelli, questuanti e banditi*, pp. 28–9.

33. De Clementi, *Vivere nel latifondo*, p. 214.

34. Riall, 'Elites in Search of Authority', pp. 40–1.

35. Rizzi, *La coccarde e le campane*, p. 20.

36. A. de Clementi, 'Individualismo agrario e mentalità communitaria in un villagio del Lazio', *Quaderni Storici*, 21 (1986), p. 934.

37. M. Malatesta, 'Il concetto della sociabilità nella storia politica italiana dell'Ottocento', in *Dimensioni e problemi della ricerca storica*, 1 (1992), pp. 59–71.

38. E. Hobsbawm, *Bandits*, 2nd edition (Harmondsworth, 1985).

39. P. Ginsborg, 'After the Revolution: Bandits on the Plains of the Po

1848–54', in Davis and Ginsborg (eds), *Society and Politics in the Age of the Risorgimento*, pp. 128–51.

40. M. Petrusewicz, 'Society against the State: Peasant Brigandage in Southern Italy', *Criminal Justice History*, 8 (1987), pp. 1–20.

41. U. Levra, *L'altro volto di Torino risorgimentale, 1814–1848* (Turin, 1989), p. 48.

42. S. J. Woolf, 'Segregazione sociale e attività politica nelle città italiane, 1815–1848', in E. Son (ed.), *Città e controllo sociale in Italia tra XVIII e XIX secolo* (Milan, 1982), p. 22.

43. M. Gibson, *Prostitution and the State in Liberal Italy* (New Brunswick, NJ, 1986), p. 16.

44. S. Ortaggi Cammarosano, 'Labouring Women in Northern and Central Italy in the Nineteenth Century', in Davis and Ginsborg (eds), *Society and Politics in the Age of the Risorgimento*, pp. 152–83.

45. M. Barbagli, 'Marriage and the Family in Italy in the Early Nineteenth Century', in Davis and Ginsborg (eds), *Society and Politics in the Age of the Risorgimento*, p. 124.

46. Gibson, *Prostitution and the State*, p. 20.

47. M. L. Berti, 'La questione sanitaria a Cremona: problemi e provvedimenti, 1830–1880', *Storia Urbana*, 3 (1977), 71–89.

48. A. Forti Messina, 'Il colera e le condizione igenico sanitare di Napoli nel 1836–37', *Storia Urbana*, 3 (1977), p. 4; P. Preto, *Epidemia, paura e politica nell'Italia moderna* (Bari, 1987), p. 138.

49. On these armed forces see the important analyses of E. Francia, *Le baionette intelligenti. La guardia nazionale nell'Italia liberale (1848–1876)* (Bologna, 1999); and A. M. Istasia, *Il volontariato militare nel Risorgimento. La partecipazione alla guerra del 1859* (Rome, 1990).

50. Barbagli, 'Marriage and the family', pp. 122–7.

51. L. Guidi and L. Valenti, 'Malattia, povertà, devianza femminile, follia nelle istituzioni napoletane di pubblica beneficenza', in Massafra (ed.), *Il Mezzogiorno preunitario,* p. 1179.

52. S. J. Woolf, 'The Poor and How to Relieve Them: the Restoration Debate on Poverty in Italy and Europe', in Davis and Ginsborg (eds), *Society and Politics in the Age of the Risorgimento,* pp. 62–9; and Woolf, 'Segregazione sociale e attività politica nelle città italiane', pp. 26–7.

53. J. A. Davis, *Conflict and Control. Law and Order in Nineteenth-Century Italy* (London, 1988), pp. 69–71, 105–11.

54. Ibid., p. 76.

55. This point is emphasised by S. C. Hughes, *Crime, Disorder and the Risorgimento. The Politics of Policing in Bologna* (Cambridge, 1994).

5 Growth, Stagnation and Economic Difference

1. L. Cafagna, 'Introduzione', in *Dualismo e sviluppo nella storia d'Italia* (Venice, 1989), p. xii.

2. E. Sereni, *Capitalismo e mercato nazionale* (Rome, 1966). See also his earlier work, more specifically concerned with agrarian structures, *Il capitalismo nelle campagne (1860–1900)* (Turin, 1947).

3. R. Romeo, *Risorgimento e capitalismo* (Bari, 1959).

4. A. Gerschenkron, 'Rosario Romeo and the Original Accumulation of Capital', in *Economic Backwardness in Historical Perspective* (Cambridge, MA, 1966).

5. G. Federico, 'Di un nuovo modello dell'industria italiana', *Società e Storia*, 8 (1980), p. 447.

6. K. R. Greenfield, *Economics and Liberalism in the Risorgimento. A Study of Nationalism in Lombardy, 1814–1848* (Baltimore, MD, 1934), pp. 4–9.

7. A. Dewerpe, *L'Industrie aux champs. Essai sur la proto-industrialisation en Italie du nord* (Rome, 1985).

8. A. Cento Bull, 'Proto-Industrialisation, Small-Scale Capital Accumulation and Diffused Entrepreneurship: The Case of the Brianza in Lombardy (1860–1950)', *Social History*, 14 (1989), p. 179.

9. G. Mori, 'Industrie senza industrializzazione: la peninsola italiana dalla fine della dominazione francese all'unità nazionale (1815–1861)', *Studi Storici*, 30 (1989), pp. 603–35.

10. F. Ramella, *Terra e telai. Sistema di parentela e manifattura nel Biellese dell'Ottocento* (Turin, 1983); A. Cento Bull, 'The Lombard Silk Industry in the 19th Century: An Industrial Workforce in a Rural Setting', *The Italianist*, 7 (1987), pp. 99–121, and 'Proto-Industrialisation and the Brianza in Lombardy'.

11. L. Cafagna, 'La prima onda industriale' and 'I modelli interpretativi della storiografia', both in *Dualismo e sviluppo*; F. Bonelli, 'Il capitalismo italiano: linee generali di interpretazione', in *Storia d'Italia. Annali,* vol. I (Turin, 1978).

12. Cafagna, 'Introduzione', in *Dualismo e sviluppo*, pp. xxix–xlii.

13. J. Davis, 'Remapping Italy's path to the twentieth century', *Journal of Modern History,* 66/2 (1994), pp. 293–6.

14. S. Pollard, *Peaceful Conquest. The Industrialisation of Europe, 1760–1970*, (Oxford, 1981).

15. Cafagna, 'I modelli interpretativi della storiografia', in *Dualismo e sviluppo*, p. 399.

16. Mori, 'Industrie senza industrializzazione', p. 606.

17. L. de Rosa, *Iniziativa e capitale straniero nell'industria metalmeccanica del Mezzogiorno 1840–1904* (Naples, 1968).

18. E. Iachello and A. Signorelli, 'Borghesie urbane dell'Ottocento', in M. Aymard and G. Giarrizzo (eds), *Storia d'Italia. Le regioni dall'unità a oggi. La Sicilia* (Turin, 1987); R. Battaglia, *Mercanti e imprenditori in una città marittima. Il caso di Messina (1850–1900)* (Milan, 1992); F. Benigno, 'Fra mare e terra: orizzonte economico e mutamento sociale in una città meridionale. Trapani nella prima metà dell'Ottocento', in A. Massafra (ed.), *Il Mezzogiorno preunitario. Economia, società, istituzioni* (Bari, 1988).

19. R. Battaglia, 'Qualità e trasformazione del ceto mercantile siciliano a
    metà dell'Ottocento', in Massafra (ed.), *Il Mezzogiorno preunitario*.

20. M. Salvadori, *Il mito del buongoverno. La questione meridionale da Cavour
    a Gramsci* (Turin, 1960).

21. P. Bevilacqua, 'Agricoltura e storia delle campagne nel Mezzogiorno
    d'Italia', *Studi Storici*, 23 (1982), p. 676 and 'Uomini, terre, economie',
    in P. Bevilacqua and A. Placanica (eds), *Storia d'Italia. Le regioni dall'u-
    nità a oggi. La Calabria* (Turin, 1985).

22. F. Assante, 'Le trasformazioni del paesaggio agrario', in Massafra (ed.),
    Il Mezzogiorno preunitario, p. 22.

23. *Studi intorno all'economia politica* (Capolago, 1840), quoted in M.
    Petrusewicz, *Latifundium. Moral Economy and Material Life in a European
    Periphery* (Ann Arbor, MI, 1996), pp. 1–2.

24. A. Creuzé de Lesser, *Voyage en Italie et Sicile* (1806), quoted in N. Moe,
    The View from Vesuvius. Italian Culture and the Southern Question
    (Berkeley, CA, 2002), p. 37.

25. Petrusewicz, *Latifundium*, p. 5.

26. Letter to the *Times Literary Supplement* (*TLS*), 4623, 8 November 1991,
    p. 15, on Adrian Lyttleton's review article 'A New Past for the
    Mezzogiorno', *TLS*, 4618, 4 October 1991, pp. 14–15, which discusses
    revisionist interpretations of the South. For further comments, see *TLS*,
    4626, 29 November 1991, p. 19; *TLS*, 4627, 6 December 1991, p. 15;
    and *TLS*, 4630, 27 December 1991, p. 13.

27. V. Giura, 'Infrastrutture, manifatture, commercio', in Massafra (ed.), *Il
    Mezzogiorno preunitario*, p. 241.

28. This approach is especially common among Anglo-American scholars
    influenced by the linguistic turn such as Nelson Moe and John Dickie.
    For a discussion see: L. Riall, 'Which road to the South? Revisionists
    revisit the Mezzogiorno', *Journal of Modern Italian Studies*, 5. 1 (2000),
    pp. 89–100.

29. P. Bevilacqua, *Breve storia dell' Italia meridionale dall'Ottocento a oggi*
    (Rome, 1993), pp. 16–17.

30. V. Zamagni, *An Economic History of Liberal Italy* (Oxford, 1993), pp.
    21–5; A. Placanica, 'I caratteri originali' and P. Bevilacqua, 'Uomini,
    terre, economie': both in Bevilacqua and Placanica (eds), *La Calabria*.

31. J. A. Davis, 'Technology and Innovation in an Industrial latecomer:
    Italy in the Nineteenth Century', in P. Matthias and J. A. Davis (eds),
    *Innovation and Technology in Europe. From the Eighteenth Century to the
    Present Day* (Oxford, 1991).

32. J. A. Davis, 'Economy, Society and the State', in J. A. Davis (ed.), *Italy in
    the Nineteenth Century* (Oxford, 2000), pp. 246–9.

33. Mori, 'Industrie senza industrializzazione', p. 606–8.

34. L. Cafagna, 'La questione delle origini del dualismo economico ital-
    iano', in *Dualismo e sviluppo*, pp. 187, 217.

35. Mori, 'Industrie senza industrializzazione', pp. 607–8.

6 Nation, Identity and Nationalist Politics

1. For example: G. Massari, *Uomini di destra* (Turin, 1888); M. Minghetti, *I miei ricordi* (Turin, 1888–90); G. Pallavicino Trivulzio, *Memorie* (Turin, 1882–95); J. White Mario, *Vita di Garibaldi*, 3rd edn (Milan, 1882) and *Agostino Bertani e i suoi tempi* (Florence, 1888); M. Castelli, *Il conte di Cavour. Ricordi* (Turin, 1886); M. d'Azeglio (*I miei ricordi*), Florence, 1867.

2. G. H. von Treitschke, *Historische und politische Aufsätze, vornehmlich zur neuesten deutschen Geschichte* (Leipzig, 1865); M. Paléologue, *Cavour, un grand réaliste* (Paris, 1926).

3. D. Mack Smith, *Cavour and Garibaldi, 1860. A Study in Political Conflict* (Cambridge, 1985 [1954]).

4. F. Chabod, *Storia dell'idea d'Europa* (Bari, 1961); A. Omodeo, *L'opera politica del conte di Cavour, 1848–1857* (Bari, 1940). On Chabod, see S. Woolf, 'Reading Federico Chabod's *Storia dell'idea d'Europa* half a century later,' *Journal of Modern Italian Studies*, 7. 2 (2002), pp. 269–292.

5. See, for example, A. M. Ghisalberti, *Momenti e figure del Risorgimento romano* (Milan, 1965).

6. C. Lovett, *The Democratic Movement in Italy, 1830–1876* (Cambridge, MA, 1982); A. Galante Garrone, *I radicali in Italia (1849–1925)* (Milan, 1973).

7. For example, F. della Peruta, *Mazzini e i rivoluzionari italiani. Il 'partito d'azione', 1830–1845* (Milan, 1974).

8. See the critical article by A. de Francesco on Italian Jacobinism in 'L'ombra di Buonarroti. Giacobinismo e Rivoluzione francese nella storiografia italiana del dopoguerra', *Storica*, 15 (1999), pp. 7–67, and his reassessment of the Gramscian view of Cuoco as the forerunner of Risorgimento moderatism in *Vincenzo Cuoco. Una vita politica* (Rome and Bari, 1997). See also De Francesco's general discussion of the French Revolution in Italian historiography: *Mito e storiografia della 'grande rivoluzione'. La Rivoluzione francese nella cultura politica italiana del' 900* (Naples, 2006).

9. A. de Francesco, 'Ideologie e movimenti politici' in G. Sabbatucci and V. Vidotto, *Storia d'Italia. 1. Le premesse dell'unità* (Rome and Bari, 1994), p. 33.

10. G. Sabbatucci and V. Vidotto, 'Introduzione' in ibid, pp. xii, xvi.

11. This question is posed by Albert Russell Ascoli and Krystyna von Henneberg in 'Introduction: Nationalism and the uses of Risorgimento Culture' in A. R. Ascoli and K. von Henneberg (eds), *Making and Remaking Italy. The Cultivation of National Identity around the Risorgimento* (Oxford, 2001), p. 5.

12. A. M. Banti, *La nazione del Risorgimento. Parentela, santità e onore alle origini dell'Italia unita* (Torino, 2000), pp. 3–29; R. Grew, 'Culture and Society, 1796–1896', in J.A. Davis (ed.), *Italy in the Nineteenth Century* (Oxford, 2000), pp. 207–10.

13. Banti, *La nazione*, pp. 44–5.
14. A. M. Banti and P. Ginsborg, 'Per una nuova storia del Risorgimento', in A. M. Banti and P. Ginsborg (eds), *Storia d'Italia, annali 22. Il Risorgimento* (Turin, 2007), p. xxiii.
15. Banti, *La nazione*, p. 53, emphasis in original.
16. S. Patriarca, 'Indolence and Regeneration: Tropes and Tensions of Risorgimento Patriotism', in *American Historical Review*, 110. 2 (2005), pp. 380–1.
17. Banti and Ginsborg, 'Per una nuova storia', pp. xxiii–xxiv.
18. P. Ginsborg, 'Romanticismo e Risorgimento: l'io, l'amore e la nazione', in A. M. Banti and P. Ginsborg (eds), *Storia d'Italia*, pp. 6–18. Here he revives the older argument of Chabod that 'the idea of the nation rises and triumphs with the rise and triumph of that great movement of European culture, which takes the name Romanticism'. F. Chabod, *L'idea di nazione*, a cura di A. Saitta and E. Sestan, (Rome and Bari, 2007 [1961]), p. 17.
19. M. Isabella, 'Exile and Nationalism: The Case of the Risorgimento', *European History Quarterly*, 36. 4 (2006), pp. 493–520; and the same author's forthcoming monograph, *Risorgimento in exile*.
20. C. Sorba, *Teatri. L'Italia del melodrama nell'età del Risorgimento* (Bologna, 2001); A. Signorelli, *A teatro, al circolo. Socialità borghese nella Sicilia dell'Ottocento* (Rome, 2000), pp. 9–104.
21. S. Chiappini, 'La voce della martire. Dagli "evirati cantori" all'eroina romantica', in Banti and Ginsborg (eds), *Storia d'Italia*, p. 304.
22. On the concept of nation as 'imagined community' see B. Anderson, *Imagined communities* (London, 1991).
23. A. Castellani, 'Quanti erano gli italofoni nel 1861?' *Studi linguistici italiani*, 8. 1 (1982), pp. 3–26.
24. R. Romani, *L'economia politica del Risorgimento italiano* (Turin, 1994).
25. S. Patriarca, *Numbers and Nationhood. Writing Statistics in Nineteenth-Century Italy* (Cambridge, 1996), pp. 3, 125.
26. L. Guidi, 'Donne e uomini del Sud sulle vie d'esilio, 1848–1860', in Banti and Ginsborg (eds), *Storia d'Italia*, pp. 225–52 and 'Patriottismo femminile e travestimenti sulla scena risorgimentale', *Studi Storici*, 41. 2 (2000), pp. 571–87.
27. M. d'Amelia, *La mamma*, Bologna, 2005, pp. 51–90.
28. M. Bonsanti, 'Amore familiare, amore romantico e amor di patria', in Banti and Ginsborg (eds), *Storia d'Italia*, p. 139.
29. Ibid., pp. 140, 147; L. Levi d'Ancona, 'Padri e figli nel Risorgimento', ibid., pp. 153–79.
30. Ginsborg, 'Romanticismo e Risorgimento', p. 51.
31. A. Russo, 'Tra fratello e sorella: Giuseppe ed Elisabetta Ricciardi. Linguaggi, strategie, idee politiche e religiose a confronto', in I. Porciani (ed.), *Famiglia e nazione nel lungo Ottocento italiano. Modelli, strategie, reti di relazione* (Rome, 2006), pp. 83–105.

32. L. Riall, *Garibaldi. Invention of a Hero* (New Haven and London, 2007), pp. 124–7, 307–14.

33. For examples of a possible new approach, see E. Francia, '"Il nuovo Cesare è la patria". Clero e religione nel lungo quarantotto italiano', and D. Menozzi, 'I gesuiti, Pio IX e la nazione Italiana', both in Banti and Ginsborg (eds), *Storia d'Italia*, pp. 423–50, 451–78.

34. I am grateful to Maurizio Isabella for his advice on this point and the following discussion.

35. Ginsborg's 'Romanticismo e Risorgimento'; and M. Thom, 'Europa, libertà e nazioni: Cattaneo e Mazzini nel Risorgimento', in Ginsborg and Banti, *Il Risorgimento*, pp. 331–78, provide useful indications for a new approach.

36. Quoted in Ginsborg, 'Romanticismo e Risorgimento', p. 53.

37. S. Levis-Sullam, '"Dio e il popolo": la rivoluzione religiosa di Giuseppe Mazzini' in Banti and Ginsborg (eds), *Storia d'Italia*, pp. 401–22.

38. R. Sarti, 'Giuseppe Mazzini and his opponents' in Davis (ed.), *Italy in the Nineteenth Century*, p. 75.

39. M. d'Azeglio, *Things I Remember*, trans. E. R. Vincent (Oxford, 1966), pp. 310–11.

40. D. Laven, 'Mazzini, Mazzinian Conspiracy and British Politics in the 1850s', *Bollettino Storico Mantovano*, nuova serie, 2 (2003), pp. 267–82.

41. R. Sarti, *Mazzini. A life for the Religion of Politics* (Westport, CT, 1997), p. 3; D. Mack Smith, *Mazzini* (London, 1994), p. 2.

42. G. Mazzini, 'Sulla missione della stampa periodica' (1836), in G. Mazzini, *Opera politiche*, 2nd edition (Torino, 2005), p. 507.

43. *Apostolato Popolare*, no.1, 10 November 1840, p. 1.

44. 7 November 1847, 13 and 17 January 1848, *Scritti editi ed inediti di Giuseppe Mazzini*, 106 vols (Imola, 1906–90), 33, pp. 52, 242, 252.

45. Riall, *Garibaldi*, pp. 46–58.

46. Sarti, *Mazzini*, pp. 95–126; Mack Smith, *Mazzini*, pp. 20–40.

47. Quoted in R. Pesman, 'Mazzini in esilio e le inglesi', in Porciani (ed.), *Famiglia e nazione*, p. 66.

48. M. Isabella, 'Italian Exiles and British Politics before and after 1848', in S. Freitag (ed.), *Exiles from European Revolutions. Refugees in Mid-Victorian England* (Oxford, 2003), pp. 59–87.

49. S. Hazareesingh, 'Memory and Political Imagination. The Legend of Napoleon Revisited', *French History*, 18. 2 (2004), pp. 463–83.

50. 'The Martyrs for Italian Liberty. I. Attilio and Emilio Bandiera', *Scritti*, 34, pp. 27–48.

51. Mack Smith, *Mazzini*, pp. 42–3.

52. G. Albergoni, *I mestieri delle lettere tra istituzioni e mercato. Vivere e scrivere a Milano nella prima metà dell'Ottocento* (Milan, 2006); M. Berengo, *Intellettuali e librai nella Milano della Restaurazione* (Turin, 1980); U. Carpi, *Letteratura e società nella Toscana del risorgimento. Gli intellettuali dell'Antologia*, (Bari, 1974).

53. On *Fieramosca*, see L. Riall, 'The Politics of Italian Romanticism', in C. Bayley and E. Biagini (eds), *Giuseppe Mazzini and the Globalization of Democratic Nationalism, 1805–2005*. Proceedings of the British Academy, 152, (Oxford, 2008), pp. 167–86.

54. R. Romani, 'L'economia politica dei moderati, 1830–1848', *Società e Storia*, 29 (2006), pp. 21–49; F. Sofia, 'Le fonti bibliche nel primato italiano di Vincenzo Gioberti', *Società e Storia*, 27 (2004), pp. 747–62.

55. R. Grew, *A Sterner Plan for Italian Unity. The Italian National Society in the Risorgimento* (Princeton NJ, 1963), p. 105; for a complete description of the National Society's propaganda activities, ibid., pp. 101–23.

56. Ibid., p. 143.

7 Italian Unification

1. Both are in D. Mack Smith (ed.), *The Making of Italy, 1796–1866* (London, 1988 [1968]), pp. 367, 395.

2. S. Patriarca, 'Indolence and Regeneration. Tropes and Tensions of Risorgimento Patriotism', *American Historical Review*, 110. 2 (2005), pp. 380–408; see also the same author's forthcoming book, *Italian Vices* (Cambridge, 2009).

3. F. Chabod, *Storia della politica estera italiana dal 1870 al 1896. Vol. 1. Le premesse* (Bari, 1951).

4. K. Wegert, 'Contention with Civility: the State and Social Control in the German Southwest, 1760–1850', *Historical Journal,* 34 (1991), p. 361.

5. L. Riall, 'Elite Resistance to State Formation: The Case of Italy', in M. Fulbrook (ed.), *National Histories and European History* (London, 1993), pp. 59–63.

6. M. Ridolfi, *Le feste nazionali* (Bologna, 2003); C. Duggan, *Francesco Crispi. From Nation to Nationalism* (Oxford, 2002); C. Brice, *Le Vittoriano. Monumentalité publique et politique à Rome* (Rome, 1998); I. Porciani, *La festa della nazione* (Bologna, 1997); M. Baioni, *La 'religione della patria'. Musei e istituti del culto risorgimentale (1884–1918)* (Treviso, 1994); U. Levra, *Fare gli italiani. Memoria e celebrazione del Risorgimento* (Turin, 1992); B. Tobia, *Una patria per gli italiani. Spazi, itinerari, monumenti nell'Italia unita* (Rome and Bari, 1991).

7. D. Laven, 'Italy: The Idea of the Nation in the Risorgimento and Liberal Eras', in T. Baycroft and M. Hewitson (eds), *What is a Nation? Europe 1789–1915* (Oxford, 2006), pp. 258, 270.

8. C. Brice, 'La monarchia e la "religione della patria" nella costruzione dell'identità nazionale', *Memoria e Ricerca*, 13 (2003), p. 143. For other examples, see O. Ihl, *La fête républicaine* (Paris, 1996); G. Mosse, *The Nationalisation of the Masses. Political Symbolism and Mass Movements in Germany from the Napoleonic Wars through the Third Reich* (New York, 1975).

9. L. Riall, *Garibaldi. Invention of a Hero* (New Haven and London, 2007) pp. 364–77, 384–7, and 'Which Italy? Italian Culture and the Problem of Politics', *Journal of Contemporary History* 39 (2004), 437–46.

10. C. Brice, 'La monarchia', pp. 144, 146–7, and *La monarchie et la construction de l'identité nationale italienne, 1861–1911*, Doctorat d'État, Institut d'études politiques de Paris (2004); F. Dolci, 'L'editoria d'occasione del secondo Ottocento nella Biblioteca di storia moderna e contemporanea di Roma', in *Il mito del Risorgimento nell'Italia unita* (Milan, 1995), pp. 124–48.

11. A. M. Banti, *Storia della borghesia italiana. L'età liberale* (Rome, 1996), p. 214.

12. Useful suggestions are provided by D. Forgacs, 'Nostra patria: Revisions of the Risorgimento in the Cinema, 1925–1952', in A. R. Ascoli and K. von Henneberg (eds), *Making and Remaking Italy. The Cultivation of National Identity around the Risorgimento* (Oxford, 2001), pp. 257–76.

13. See the perceptive comments of Laura Guidi, 'Patriottismo femminile e travestimenti sulla scena risorgimentale', *Studi Storici*, 41. 2 (2000), pp. 571–87; and for an analysis of women writers: L. Re, 'Passion and Sexual Difference: The Risorgimento and the Gendering of Writing in Nineteenth-Century Italian Culture', in Ascoli and Henneberg (eds), *Making and Remaking Italy*, pp. 155–200.

14. R. Grew, 'Catholicism and the Risorgimento', in F. Coppa (ed.), *Studies in Modern Italian History. From the Risorgimento to the Republic* (New York, 1986), p. 50. See also P. Burke, 'Perceiving a counter-culture' in P. Burke, *The Historical Anthropology of Early-Modern Italy* (Cambridge, 1987), pp. 63–79.

A Guide to Further Reading

There is a large number of narrative histories of the Risorgimento and Italian unification. Of the more recent works, perhaps the most complete is D. Beales and E. F. Biagini, *The Risorgimento and the Unification of Italy* (London, 2002 [1971]), a wide-ranging history with a selection of original documents. Chapters 1 to 10 of C. Duggan, *The Force of Destiny. A History of Italy since 1796* (London, 2007) cover the Risorgimento. A. M. Banti, *Il Risorgimento Italiano* (Rome and Bari, 2004) is an innovative account from the Risorgimento's foremost cultural historian, but is unfortunately not translated into English. The essays in J. A. Davis (ed.), *Italy in the Nineteenth Century* (Oxford, 2000) provide a good introduction to the themes and narratives of Risorgimento history. D. Mack Smith (ed), *The Making of Italy, 1796–1886* (London, 1988 [1968]), is a collection of documents on the Risorgimento.

For a more detailed narrative which concentrates on the social history of the period, see S. J. Woolf, A *History of Italy, 1700–1860. The Social Constraints of Political Change* (London, 1979), while H. Hearder, *Italy in the Age of the Risorgimento* (London, 1983) and F. J. Coppa, *The Origins of the Italian Wars of Independence* (London, 1992) are also useful (Coppa focuses on the diplomatic and military aspects of unification). J. A. Davis, *Conflict and Control. Law and Order in Nineteenth-Century Italy* (London, 1988) is a valuable introduction to the subject of law and order and is helpful as a broad guide to the social history of Italy. In Italian, Giorgio Candeloro's multi-volume *Storia dell'Italia moderna* (Milan, 1956–78), written from a Marxist perspective, is still of real use (volumes 1 to 5 cover the Risorgimento and national unification), while A. Scirocco, *L'Italia del Risorgimento* (Bologna, 1990) is a clear narrative with some good detail.

Introductions to historiographical issues can be found in the introductory chapter of Beales and Biagini, *The Risorgimento and the Unification of Italy* and chapter 1 of Hearder, *Italy in the Age of the Risorgimento*. Those wishing to investigate further should consult S. J. Woolf (ed.), *The Italian Risorgimento* (London, 1969), especially the introduction and part II. Readers can get a sense of the historical controversies over the Risorgimento and Italian unification by comparing Benedetto Croce's *A History of Italy, 1871–1915,* translated by C. M. Ady (Oxford, 1929), with Antonio Gramsci's 'Notes on Italian history', in *Selections from the Prison Notebooks of Antonio Gramsci*, edited and translated by. Q. Hoare and G. Nowell Smith (London, 1971).

For an interesting and accessible analysis of Croce as a historian and politician, see D. Mack Smith, 'Benedetto Croce', *Journal of Contemporary History*, 8 (1973), pp. 41–61. The main ideas behind the post-war Anglo-American approach to the Risorgimento are well presented in the author's introduction to the second edition of D. Mack Smith, *Cavour and Garibaldi, 1860. A Study in Political Conflict* (Cambridge, 1985 [1954]); H. Stuart Hughes, 'The Aftermath of the Risorgimento in Four Successive Interpretations', *American Historical Review*, 61. 1 (1955), pp. 70–6; and A. W. Salamone (ed.), *Italy from Liberalism to Fascism. An Inquiry into the Origins of the Totalitarian State* (New York, 1970). In Italian, a fairly exhaustive bibliography to the Risorgimento is provided by *Bibliografia dell'età del Risorgimento*, 4 volumes (Florence, 2003) (although its organisation is far from user-friendly).

For more up-to-date discussions, dealing specifically with the 'revisionist' approach but focusing more on the period after unification, John Davis's 'Remapping Italy's Path to the Twentieth Century', *Journal of Modern History*, 66. 2, (1994), pp. 291–320, is particularly helpful. It is also useful as a general introduction to debates about Restoration government, Italian society and economic development. Some discussion of the revisionist agenda, but again focusing on the period after unification, is provided by Raffaele Romanelli, 'Political Debate, Social History and the Italian *borghesia*: Changing Perspectives in Historical Research', *Journal of Modern History*, 63. 4 (1991), pp. 717–39. In Italian: the 'afterword' to Franco Rizzi's *La coccarda e le campane. Comunità rurali e repubblica romana nel Lazio (1848–1849)* (Milan, 1989), the introduction to Paolo Macry's *Ottocento. Famiglia, élites e patrimoni a Napoli* (Turin, 1988), and the introduction by editors Giovanni Sabbatucci and Vittorio Vidotto to *Storia d'Italia. 1. Le premesse dell'unità dalla fine del settecento al 1861* (Rome and Bari, 1994) are important as position statements from 'revisionist' historians.

There has been a great interest in new historical approaches to southern Italy among Anglo-Saxon scholars, although again most of it has focused on the post-1860 period. The editors' introductions and essays in the two volumes: J. Morris and R. Lumley (eds), *The New History of the Italian South. The Mezzogiorno Revisited* (Exeter, 1997) and J. Schneider (ed.), *Italy's "Southern Question". Orientalism in One Country* (Oxford, 1998) offer a guide to, and sample of, the new literature, while M. Petrusewicz, *Latifundium. Moral Economy and Material Life in a European Periphery* (Ann Arbor, MI, 1996) makes the case for a new historical understanding of the Southern landed estates. N. Moe, *The View from Vesuvius. Italian Culture and the Southern Question* (Berkeley and Los Angeles, CA, 2002) looks at the construction of the 'Southern Question'. There is a good analysis of recent literature in E. dal Lago, 'Rethinking the Bourbon Kingdom', *Modern Italy*, 6. 1 (2001), pp. 69–78, while L. Riall, 'Which Road to the South? Revisionists Revisit the Mezzogiorno', *Journal of Modern Italian Studies*, 5. 1 (2000), pp. 89–100, assesses the new Southern historiography, focusing on attempts to apply Edward Said's theory of 'Orientalism' to the Mezzogiorno. A. Lyttleton, 'A New Past for the Mezzogiorno', in *Times Literary Supplement* (4 October 1991), 4618, pp. 14–15 reviews Petrusewicz's ground-breaking work. In Italian, Piero Bevilacqua's introduction to his *Breve storia dell'Italia meridionale dall'Ottocento a oggi* (Rome, 1993), is a concise statement of the revisionist approach to the South from a leading economic historian. Franco Benigno's introduction to F. Benigno and C. Torrisi, *Elites e potere in Sicilia dal medioevo ad oggi* (Rome, 1995) lays down a challenge to the 'dualistic' categories used to explain Southern 'backwardness'.

On Restoration government and the legacy of Napoleon, see the introduction by David Laven and Lucy Riall to *Napoleon's Legacy. Problems of Government in Restoration Europe* (Oxford, 2000), pp. 1–26, and on the complex forms of political conflict during the Restoration, see M. Meriggi, 'State and Society in Post-Napoleonic Italy' in the same volume. Hearder's *Italy in the Age of the Risorgimento* has a lot of detail on Restoration government but his analysis overemphasises the reactionary elements. David Laven has written a vigorous rehabilitation of the Austrian government in Venetia during the early Restoration period: *Venice and Venetia under the Habsburgs, 1815–1835* (Cambridge, 2002) and has also challenged traditional views of Austria's Italian policy, focusing on international politics ('Austria's Italian Policy Reconsidered: Revolution and Reform in Restoration Italy', *Modern Italy*, 3 in 1997), pp. 3–33. The case for a new approach to Restoration Piedmont is made by Michael Broers, 'The Restoration in Piedmont-Sardinia, 1814–1848: Variations on Reaction' in Laven and Riall (eds), *Napoleon's Legacy*, pp. 151–64. Those wishing to know more about the relations between popular classes and the Restoration governments should start with A. J. Reinerman, 'The Failure of Popular Counter-Revolution in Risorgimento Italy: The Case of the Centurions, 1831–1847', *The Historical Journal,* 34 (1991), pp. 21–41.

There are a series of studies in English of the Church in Napoleonic and Restoration Italy. Especially important on the origins of the conflict between Church and state is M. Broers, *The Politics of Religion in Napoleonic Italy. The War against God, 1801–1814* (London, 2002). A. J. Reinerman, *Austria and the Papacy in the Age of Metternich,* 2 vols (Washington, DC, 1979–89) contains good discussions of Metternich's Italian policy and the problem of the papacy. Frank Coppa's study of *Cardinal Giacomo Antonelli and Papal Politics in European Affairs* (Albany, NY, 1990) offers some fascinating insights into the career of Pius IX's secretary of state, and indicates that Antonelli's reputation as a reactionary needs to be modified. A significant part of O. Chadwick, *The Popes and European Revolution* (Oxford, 1981) is concerned with Italy: Chapter 8 deals with the Restoration period.

Unfortunately, since so little historical research in Italy has been translated into English, a knowledge of Italian is essential if specific subjects are to be studied in any detail. The revisionist approach to Restoration government in northern and central Italy is represented in two studies of pre-unification Italy published by UTET of Turin: M. Caravale and A. Caracciolo, *Lo Stato Pontificio da Martino V a Pio X* (Turin, 1978) and M. Meriggi, *Il regno Lombardo-Veneto* (Turin, 1987). Marco Meriggi also redefines the relationship between the Lombard élites and the Austrian administration in *Amministrazione e classi sociali nel Lombardo-Veneto 1814–1848* (Bologna, 1983), providing a wealth of information about the effect of administrative centralisation on relations between classes, and between state and society. On the reforms of Carlo Alberto in Piedmont, the most important study to have appeared in recent years is N. Nada, *Dallo stato assoluto allo stato costituzionale. Storia del regno di Carlo Alberto dal 1831 al 1848* (Turin, 1980), which seeks to 'rescue' Carlo Alberto from the negative judgements of nationalist historiography. On the Duchy of Parma, see: B. Montale, *Parma nel Risorgimento: istituzioni e società (1814–1859)* (Milan, 1993).

There is now a significant body of work on the Risorgimento in southern Italy. A study of government in the Napoleonic period which has important implications for our understanding of the South as a whole is J. A. Davis, *Naples and Napoleon. Southern Italy and the European Revolutions, 1780–1860* (Oxford, 2006). For Sicily, the first four chapters of L. Riall, *Sicily and the Unification of Italy, 1859–1866. Liberal Policy and Local Power* (Oxford, 1998) look at the Risorgimento. The effects of land reform on state–elite relations, on relations between rival elites in Sicily and on relations between landowners and peasants are examined by L. Riall, 'Elites in Search of Authority: Political Power and Social Order in Nineteenth-Century Sicily', *History Workshop Journal*, 55 (2003), pp. 25–46. Older but still useful is D. Mack Smith, *A History of Sicily. Modern Sicily after 1713* (New York, 1968), chapters 40–6.

Those wishing to pursue further research will again have to rely on Italian language material. A. Spagnoletti, *Storia del Regno delle Due Sicilie* (Bologna, 1997) and V. d'Alessandro and G. Giarrizzo, *La Sicilia dal vespro al'unità d'Italia* (Turin, 1989) are excellent general outlines. On the problems of government in the South, and relations between state and society, see A. Scirocco, 'L'amministrazione civile: istituzioni, funzionari, carriere', and A. Spagnoletti, 'Centri e periferie nello stato napoletano del primo ottocento', both in A. Massafra (ed.), *Il Mezzogiorno preunitario: economia, società, istituzioni* (Bari, 1988). P. Pezzino, 'Monarchia amministrativa ed *élites* locali: Naro nella prima metà dell'ottocento,' in P. Pezzino, *Un paradiso abitato dai diavoli. Società, élites, istituzioni nel Mezzogiorno contemporaneo* (Milan, 1992) looks at the conflicts between central and local power in one Sicilian community.

For general introductory surveys of Italian society in this period, see Woolf, *A History of Italy,* and Davis, *Conflict and Control*. Although many of the findings in K. R. Greenfield, *Economics and Liberalism in the Risorgimento. A Study of Nationalism in Lombardy, 1814–1848* (Baltimore, MD, 1934) have been challenged, it is still useful as a general account of social and economic change in Lombardy. John Davis, 'Introduction: Antonio Gramsci and Italy's Passive Revolution' and P. Ginsborg, 'Gramsci and the Era of Bourgeois Revolution in Italy', both in J. A. Davis (ed.), *Gramsci and Italy's Passive Revolution* (London, 1979) are critical analyses of the Risorgimento as 'passive revolution'. For a history of the Risorgimento as a failed bourgeois revolution, see L. Cafagna, 'Se il risorgimento italiano sia stato una "rivoluzione borghese"', in L. Cafagna, *Dualismo e sviluppo nella storia d'Italia* (Venice, 1989).

There is a substantial literature on elites and middle classes in nineteenth-century Italy. A. Lyttleton, 'The Middle Classes in Liberal Italy', in J. A. Davis and P. Ginsborg (eds), *Society and Politics in the Age of the Risorgimento* (Cambridge, 1991) is a very good introduction, although it concentrates on the later nineteenth century. Of the literature in Italian, the most important works are Macry, *Ottocento* (on aristocratic families in Naples), and A. M. Banti, *Terra e denaro. Una borghesia padana dell'Ottocento* (Venice, 1989) (on the agrarian bourgeoisie of Piacenza). M. Meriggi, 'La borghesia italiana', in J. Kocka (ed.), *Borghesie europee dell'Ottocento* (Venice, 1989) includes a discussion of the Italian bourgeoisie prior to unification. There are a number of local studies of the new associational life of urban elites in A. M. Banti and M. Meriggi (eds), 'Elites e associazioni nell'Italia dell'Ottocento', *Quaderni Storici*, 77. 2 (1991) and M. Meriggi, *Milano borghese. Circoli ed élites nell'Ottocento* (Venice, 1993); there are also some local studies of southern elites in Massafra (ed.), *Il Mezzogiorno preunitario*.

The complex life of the landed classes and nobility throughout Italy, before and after unification, has been revealed in a series of studies, perhaps most notably in E. dal Lago, *Agrarian Elites. American Slaveholders and Southern Italian Landowners, 1815–1861* (Baton Rouge, LA, 2005); T. Kroll, *La rivolta del patriziato. Il liberalismo della nobiltà nella Toscana del Risorgimento* (Florence, 2005); A. L. Cardoza, *Aristocrats in Bourgeois Italy. The Piedmontese Nobility, 1861–1930* (Cambridge, 1997); and G. Montroni, *Gli uomini del Re. La nobiltà napoletana nell'Ottocento* (Rome, 1996).

For an analysis of the peasant unrest and elite conflict which led to the infamous revolt in Bronte, Sicily in 1860, see L. Riall, 'Nelson versus Bronte: Land, Litigation and Local Politics in Sicily, 1799–1860', *European History Quarterly*, 29. 1 (1999), pp. 39–73. Paul Ginsborg looks at the forms and repression of banditry in Venetia in 'After the Revolution: Bandits on the Plains of the Po 1848–54', while Giovanna Fiume analyses the relations between bandits and local power in Sicily in 'Bandits, Violence and the Organisation of Power in Sicily in the Early Nineteenth Century': both are in Davis and Ginsborg (eds), *Society and Politics in the Age of the Risorgimento*, pp. 70–91, 128–51. For an innovative analysis of the relationship between bandits and the state see M. Petrusewicz, 'Society against the State: Peasant Brigandage in Southern Italy', *Criminal Justice History* 8 (1987), pp. 1–20. In Italian, P. Brunello, *Ribelli, questuanti e banditi. Proteste contadine in Veneto e in Friuli, 1814–1866* (Venice, 1981), A. de Clementi, *Vivere nel latifondo. Le comunità della campagna laziale fra '700 e '800* (Milan, 1989) and M. Caffiero, 'Usi e abusi: comunità rurali e difesa dell'economia tradizionale nello stato pontificio', *Passato e Presente*, 24 (1990), pp. 73–93 look at rural life, and the impact of social and economic change in local communities. Those interested in the variety of approaches to criminality in Southern Italy should also look at the contributions in Massafra (ed.), *Il Mezzogiorno preunitario*.

On responses to poverty and charitable institutions, see S. J. Woolf, 'The Poor and How to Relieve Them: The Restoration Debate on Poverty in Italy and Europe', and M. Barbagli, 'Marriage and the Family in Italy in the Early Nineteenth Century'. Both are in Davis and Ginsborg (eds), *Society and Politics in the Age of the Risorgimento*, pp. 49–69, 92–127. The same volume also contains an invaluable general survey of women and work by Simonetta Ortaggi Cammarosano, 'Labouring Women in Northern and Central Italy in the Nineteenth Century', pp. 152–83. Steven Hughes's study of policing in Bologna, *Crime, Disorder and the Risorgimento. The Politics of Policing in Bologna* (Cambridge, 1994) is a very revealing study of urban crime and disorder, and their effect on relations between state and society. Mary Gibson, *Prostitution and the State in Liberal Italy* (New Brunswick, NJ, 1986) is an excellent general history of prostitution and has some useful information on the Risorgimento period.

In Italian, G. Pescosolido, *L'economia e la vita materiale*, in Sabbatucci and Vidotto (eds), *Storia d'Italia*, vol. I, pp. 3–118 is an up-to-date synthesis of social conditions. E. Sori (ed.), *Città e controllo sociale in Italia tra XVIII e XIX secolo* (Milan, 1982) is perhaps the best place to start reading about the conditions of the urban poor. More general information about conditions in the capital cities of Restoration Italy is in *Le città capitale degli stati pre-unitari. Atti del LIII Congresso del Istituto per la Storia del Risorgimento Italiano. 1986* (Rome, 1988). P. Preto, *Epidemia, paura e politica nell'Italia moderna* (Bari, 1987) has a good general discussion of the effect of epidemics in urban centres. U. Levra, *L'altro volto del Torino risorgimentale. 1814–1848* (Turin, 1989) studies the conditions of the urban poor, relations between classes and forms of social control in Turin.

On economic development, the best starting-point is L. Cafagna, 'The Industrial Revolution in Italy, 1830–1914', in C. Cipolla (ed.), *The Fontana Economic History of Europe*, vol. IV (London, 1973). Readers with a knowledge of Italian may also wish to consult the collection of his essays on Italian economic development: *Dualismo e sviluppo nella storia d'Italia*. V. Zamagni, *An Economic History of Liberal Italy* (Oxford, 1993) and G. Toniolo, *An Economic History of Liberal Italy 1850–1918* (London, 1990) are good overviews but with little on the Risorgimento.

E. Sereni, *Il capitalismo nelle campagne (1860–1900)* (Turin, 1947) and R. Romeo, *Risorgimento e capitalismo* (Bari, 1959) give a sense of the ferocity of the debate between Marxists and liberals at this time. Woolf (ed.), *The Italian Risorgimento*, and C. F. Delzell (ed.), *The Unification of Italy, 1859–1861. Cavour, Mazzini or Garibaldi?* (New York, 1965) have English extracts from Romeo's book, while Sereni's *A History of the Italian Agricultural Landscape* (Princeton, NJ, 1997) provides something of an introduction in English to his historical work. A. Gerschenkron, 'Rosario Romeo and the Original Accumulation of Capital' in A. Gerschenkron, *Economic Backwardness in Historical Perspective* (Cambridge, MA, 1966) is a further contribution to this debate. Much of Cafagna's work represents an attempt to get away from this debate, as does F. Bonelli's 'Il capitalismo italiano: linee generali di interpretazione', in *Storia d'Italia, Annali,* vol. I, (Turin, 1978). On Bonelli's work, see G. Federico, 'Di un nuovo modello dell'industria italiana', *Società e Storia,* 8 (1980), pp. 433–55.

Anna Bull has written two interesting and critical contributions to the proto-industrialisation debate, 'The Lombard Silk Spinners in the 19th Century; an Industrial Workforce in a Rural Setting', *The Italianist,* 7 (1987), pp. 99–121, and 'Proto-Industrialisation, Small-Scale Capital Accumulation and Diffused Entrepreneurship: The Case of Brianza in Lombardy (1860–1950)', *Social History,* 14 (1989), pp. 177–200. The first two chapters of A. Bull and P. Corner, *From Peasant to Entrepreneur. The Survival of the Family Economy in Italy* (Oxford, 1993) are an extremely useful introduction to debates about the peasant economy in Italy during this period. Other important articles on proto-industrialisation in Italy, are G. Mori, 'Il tempo della protoindustrializzazione' in G. Mori (ed.), *L'industrializzazione in Italia* (Bologna, 1981) and the same author's 'Industrie senza industrializzazione: la peninsola italiana dalla fine della dominazione francese all'unità nazionale (1815–1861)', *Studi Storici,* 30 (1989), pp. 603–35. F. Ramella, *Terra e telai. Sistema di parentela e manifattura nel Biellese dell'Ottocento* (Turin, 1983) uses the proto-industrial model for this 'micro' study of industry and kinship structures in Biella (Lombardy). On technology, see J. A. Davis, 'Technology and Innovation in an Industrial Latecomer: Italy in the Nineteenth Century', in P. Matthias and J. A. Davis (eds), *Innovation and Technology in Europe. From the Eighteenth Century to the Present Day* (Oxford, 1991).

On the Sicilian *latifondo,* see L. Riall, '"Ill-contrived, badly executed [and] . . . of no avail"? Reform and its impact in the Sicilian *latifondo* (c.1770–c.1910)', in R. Halpern and E. dal Lago (eds), *The American South and the Italian Mezzogiorno: Essays in Comparative History* (London, 2002). Denis Mack Smith has also written an interesting essay, 'The Latifundia in Modern Sicilian History', *Proceedings of the British Academy,* 51 (1965), pp. 85–124. For a classic statement of the backwardness of Southern agriculture, see M. Rossi Doria, 'The Land Tenure System and Class in Southern Italy', *American Historical Review,* 64. 1 (1958), pp. 46–53. For a more positive assessment of the latifondo, and as an antidote to the negative views of Mack Smith and Doria, see Petrusewicz, *Latifundum* (in English), and P. Bevilacqua, 'Uomini, terre, economie' in P. Bevilacqua and A. Placanica (eds), *Storia d' Italia. Le regioni dall'unità a oggi. La Calabria* (Turin, 1985) (in Italian). More generally, on industry, agriculture and trade in the South, the best starting-point is the contributions to Massafra (ed.), *Il Mezzogiorno preunitario.*

There is a vast literature on nationalist politics in the Risorgimento, and the political struggles of the Risorgimento have attracted a lot of attention from English-speaking scholars. P. Ginsborg *Daniele Manin and the Venetian Revolution of 1848–1849* (Cambridge, 1979), despite its regional focus, is useful as a general study of democratic politics in these years. C. Lovett, *The Democratic Movement in Italy, 1830–1876* (Cambridge, MA, 1982) is a biographical and statistical study of radical activists; of central importance on the radicals (in Italian) is A. Galante Garrone, *I radicali in Italia (1849–1925)* (Milan, 1973). For a reassessment of Mazzini's contribution to Italian nationalism, see L. Riall, 'The Politics of Italian Romanticism', in C. Bayley and E. Biagini (eds), *Giuseppe Mazzini and the Globalization of Democratic Nationalism, 1805–2005. Proceedings of the British Academy*, 152 (Oxford, 2008), pp. 167–86, as well as other contributions to the same volume. R. Grew, *A Sterner Plan for Italian Unity. The Italian National Society in the Risorgimento* (Princeton, NJ, 1963) is a fascinating study of the National Society, which points towards the new cultural approach to the Risorgimento which has emerged in more recent years.

On the events of 1860, the classic study is Mack Smith, *Cavour and Garibaldi*. Both Mack Smith (*Mazzini*, New Haven and London, 1994) and Roland Sarti (*Mazzini. A life for the Religion of Politics*, Westport and London, 1997) have published biographies of Mazzini; while Mack Smith's *Cavour* (London, 1985), written from a very critical perspective, is useful as an introductory biography. The most complete biography of Cavour is Rosario Romeo's *Cavour e il suo tempo*, 3 vols (Bari, 1969–84).

The 'new cultural history' of the Risorgimento is also quite well-represented in the English-speaking world. S. Patriarca, 'Indolence and Regeneration: Tropes and Tensions of Risorgimento Patriotism', *American Historical Review*, 110. 2 (2005), pp. 380–408 and M. Isabella, 'Exile and Nationalism: The Case of the Risorgimento', *European History Quarterly*, 36. 4 (2006), pp. 493–520 are important contributions to this new approach to Italian nationalism. L. Riall, *Garibaldi. Invention of a Hero* (New Haven and London, 2007) investigates the cult of Garibaldi using a cultural history framework. A. Lyttelton, 'The National Question in Italy', in M. Teich and R. Porter (eds), *The National Question in Europe in Historical Context* (Cambridge 1993) was one of the earliest attempts to adopt a fresh perspective on Italian national identity, while the same author's 'Creating a National Past: History, Myth and Image in the Risorgimento', in A. Russell Ascoli and K. von Henneberg (eds), *Making and Remaking Italy. The Cultivation of National Identity around the Risorgimento* (Oxford, 2001), pp. 27–74 is an absorbing study of Risorgimento myths and narratives and their changing uses; the whole volume is a varied and valuable addition to the growing field of cultural studies of nationalism.

Otherwise, the main contributions to the 'new cultural history' of the Risorgimento are only available in Italian. The central text is A. M. Banti, *La nazione del Risorgimento. Parentela, santità e onore alle origini dell'Italia unita*

(Turin, 2000); however, Banti has published two shorter pieces in English: 'Conclusions: Performative Effects and "deep images" in National Discourse' in L. Cole (ed.), *Different Paths to the Nation. Regional and National Identities in Central Europe and Italy, 1830–1870* (London, 2007), pp. 220–9 and 'Sacrality and the Aesthetics of Politics: Mazzini's Concept of the Nation' in Bayley and Biagini (eds), *Giuseppe Mazzini and the Globalization of Democratic Nationalism*, pp. 59–74. The most complete statement of the cultural approach to nationalism is in A. M. Banti and P. Ginsborg (eds), *Storia d'Italia. Annali 22. Il Risorgimento* (Turin, 2007). The volume contains a wealth of innovative articles by established and younger scholars and will provide the benchmark for future research on the Risorgimento. Also important for the new cultural history of the Risorgimento are: A. M. Banti and R. Bizzocchi (eds), *Immagini della nazione nell'Italia del Risorgimento* (Rome, 2002).

The new cultural history of the Risorgimento also intersects and overlaps with new research on the history of gender and family, and on scientific and associational life in the Risorgimento and after. There is a substantial section in Banti and Ginsborg (eds), *Il Risorgimento* dedicated to gender; other important studies include: I. Porciani (ed.), *Famiglia e nazione nel lungo Ottocento Italiano* (Rome, 2006), M. D'Amelia, *La mamma* (Bologna, 2005), L. Guidi, 'Patriottismo femminile e travestimenti sulla scena risorgimentale', *Studi Storici*, 41. 2 (2000), 571–87, S. Soldani, 'Donne e nazione nella rivoluzione italiana del 1848', *Passato e Presente*, 17 (1999), pp. 75–102, R. de Longis, 'Le donne hanno avuto un Risorgimento?', *Memoria*, 21 (1991), pp. 80–91.

The scientific, artistic and intellectual life of Risorgimento Italy has also received renewed attention. S. Patriarca, *Numbers and Nationhood: Writing Statistics in Nineteenth Century Italy* (Cambridge, 1996) looks at statistical 'imaginings' of the Italian nation; C. Sorba, *Teatri. L'Italia del melodramma nell'età del Risorgimento* (Bologna, 2001) examines the role of theatre and music. G. Albergoni, *I mestieri delle lettere tra istituzioni e mercato. Vivere e scrivere a Milano nella prima metà dell'Ottocento* (Milan, 2006) is a history of reading and readers, and of literary and cultural production in early Risorgimento Milan; M. Berengo, *Intellettuali e librai nella Milano della Restaurazione* (Turin, 1980) is the key work on intellectual life and publishing.

On Risorgimento journalism, still fundamental is A. Galante Garrrone and F. della Peruta, *La stampa italiana del Risorgimento* (Bari, 1976). In English, Grew, *A Sterner Plan for Italian Unity* is extremely useful on the publishing ventures of the National Society, and Riall, *Garibaldi*, chapter 5 considers the relationship between print culture and the cult of Garibaldi.

A number of new studies of the political economy and political thought in the Risorgimento have been published since the 1990s, and these have added depth and complexity to our knowledge of moderate liberalism. In English, Maurizio Isabella's forthcoming volume *Risorgimento in Exile* is an important and innovative study of the intellectual origins of moderate liberalism. In Italian, see in particular R. Romani, *L'economia politica del Risorgimento Italiano* (Torino, 1994) and E. Di Ciommo, *La nazione possibile. Mezzogiorno e questione nazionale nel 1848* (Milan, 1993). U. Carpi, 'Egemonia moderata e intellettuali nel Risorgimento', in *Storia d'Italia, Annali, 4, Intelletuali e potere* (Turin, 1981) is a good introduction to moderate liberalism.

There are a number of English-language studies of Italy after unification. Duggan, *The Force of Destiny*, chapters 11–19, offers a good survey of the problems of liberal Italy, while C. Seton Watson, *Italy from Liberalism to Fascism* (London, 1968) is a very detailed narrative history. Mack Smith has written a controversial history of Italy after unification, *Italy: A Modern History* (New Haven and London, 1997 [1959]), which stresses the disappointments of the 'post-Risorgimento'. M. Clark, *Modern Italy, 1871–1995* (London, 1996) is a general textbook. For an analysis of the problems of state formation, see L. Riall, 'Elite Resistance to State Formation: The Case of Italy', in M. Fulbrook (ed.), *National Histories and European history* (London, 1993).

In Italian, R. Romanelli, *L'Italia liberale* (Bologna, 1979) is a good survey, as are the essays in *Storia d'Italia. Vol. 2. Il nuovo Stato e la società civile*, G. Sabbatucci and V. Vidotto (eds) (Rome and Bari,1995). On political life after 1860, see F. Cammarano, *Storia politica dell'Italia liberale, 1861–1901* (Rome and Bari, 1999) and A. Berselli, *Il governo della Destra. Italia legale e Italia reale dopo l'Unità* (Bologna, 1997). A. M. Banti, *Storia della borghesia italiana. L'età liberale* (Rome, 1996) is a good social history of the period.

There are numerous studies of attempts to 'make Italians' after unification, on the construction of a 'civic religion' and on the use of the Risorgimento as a 'foundation story'. These revolve largely around the question of success or failure. C. Duggan, *Francesco Crispi, 1818–1901. From Nation to Nationalism* (Oxford, 2002), especially chapters 9–15, is the most complete study in English. For a shorter article on the same subject, see C. Duggan, 'Nation-Building in Nineteenth-Century Italy: The Case of Francesco Crispi', *History Today*, 52 (February, 2002). D. Laven, 'Italy. The Idea of the Nation in the Risorgimento and Liberal Era', in T. Baycroft and M. Hewitson (eds), *What Is a Nation? Europe 1789–1914* (Oxford, 2006), pp. 255–71 makes a harsh judgement about the process of making Italians. Riall, *Garibaldi*, chs. 11–12, discusses the 'post-Risorgimento' experience of Garibaldi in terms of 'making Italians' and argues that the question of success and failure is a misleading one.

M. Ridolfi, C. Brice and F. de Giorgi, 'Religione civile e identità nazionale nella storia d'Italia: per una discussione', *Memoria e Ricerca*, 13 (2003), pp. 133–52 also outline a more positive perspective. Other key works include: M. Ridolfi, *Le feste nazionali* (Bologna, 2003); C. Brice, *Le Vittoriano. Monumentalité publique et politique à Rome*, (Rome, 1998); I. Porciani, *La festa della nazione* (Bologna, 1997); *Il mito del Risorgimento nell'Italia unita* (Milan, 1995); M. Baioni, *La 'religione della patria'. Musei e istituti del culto risorgi-*

Index